Merry Christmas Jacki
Here is to many meals together!
Love Audra

the

wellness
mama
cookbook

the
wellness
mama
cookbook

200 easy-to-prepare recipes
and time-saving advice for the busy cook

KATIE WELLS

HARMONY BOOKS
NEW YORK

Published in the United States by Harmony
Books, an imprint of the Crown Publishing Group,
a division of Penguin Random House LLC,
New York.
crownpublishing.com

Harmony Books is a registered trademark, and
the Circle colophon is a trademark of Penguin
Random House LLC.

Wellness Mama¹ and the Wellness Mama logo
are trademarks/service marks of Wellnessmama.com.

A previous edition was self-published in the
United States by Wellness Media, Rockfield, KY, in 2014.

Library of Congress Cataloging-in-Publication Data
Names: Wells, Katie (Blogger), author.
Title: The Wellness Mama cookbook / Katie Wells.
Description: First edition. | New York : Harmony Books,
[2016] | Includes index.
Identifiers: LCCN 2016016419| ISBN 9780451496911 |
ISBN 9780451496928 (eBook)
Subjects: LCSH: Cooking (Natural foods) | Nutrition. |
Health. | LCGFT: Cookbooks.
Classification: LCC TX741 .W456 2016 |
DDC 641.3/02--dc23 LC record available at
https://lccn.loc.gov/2016016419

ISBN 978-0-451-49691-1
eBook ISBN 978-0-451-49692-8

Printed in China

Book design by La Tricia Watford
Photographs by Helene Dujardin
Jacket design by La Tricia Watford
Jacket photograph by Helene Dujardin

10 9 8 7 6 5 4 3 2 1

First Harmony Books Edition

TO MY HUSBAND & CHILDREN

You are the reason that I write, cook, and care about the future
of our world. I love you more than words can express.

TO MY PARENTS

For teaching me to forge my own path and to question
everything.

TO YOU

Thank you for reading this book and caring about real food
and the future we create for our children.

contents

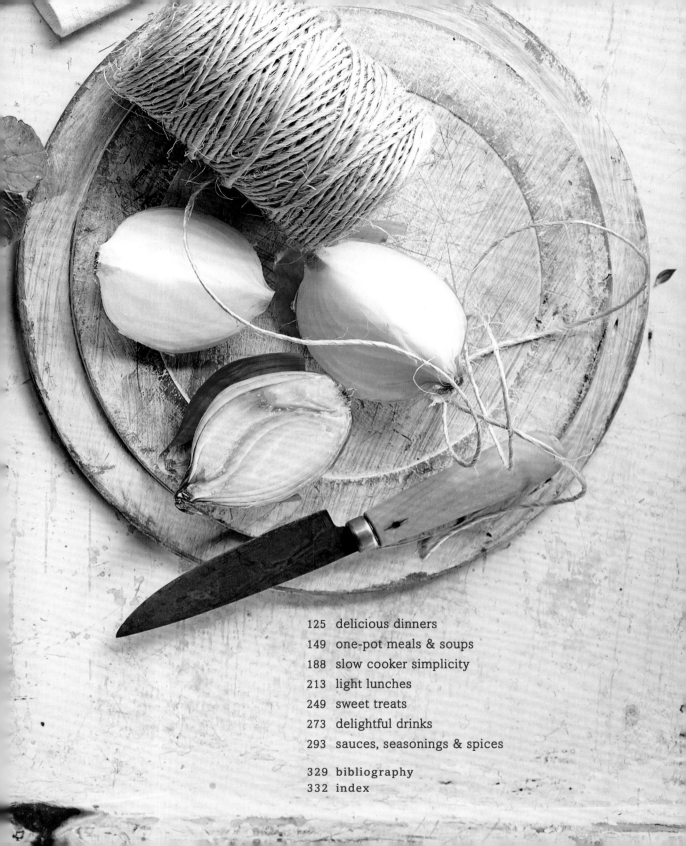

introduction

When my oldest child was just six weeks old, I was sitting in the doctor's office for a follow-up appointment and nursing him while I waited to see the doctor. His birth hadn't been what I had hoped it would be and being back at the doctor's office was a vivid reminder of that. In a way, I felt like I had failed. My water broke before contractions started and I went immediately to the hospital, where I was put "on the clock." After about twelve hours of natural labor, I was put on a two-hour timetable at only six centimeters dilated. The on-call doctor wanted to do a C-section at only twelve hours after my water broke even though there was no sign of infection or stress to the baby. I later found out that the on-call doctor had the highest C-section rate in our city.

I agreed to start pitocin to avoid the C-section if possible and ended up needing an epidural when the pain started causing me to black out.

In hindsight, there were so many things that I would have changed about that birth; but at the same time, I wouldn't have changed any of it for the world. I learned a lot about myself that day, I met my son, and my bond with my husband became even stronger. That day ignited an internal strength and passion that I didn't know I was capable of, and I developed what I called the "mother lion" instinct as soon as I saw my son.

Six weeks later in that doctor's office, as I sat nursing my little guy and mindlessly flipping through a magazine, I was still reflecting on the many emotions associated with birth and learning the ropes of caring for a newborn. In that moment, my finger stopped on a page of the magazine with a picture of a cute baby (something new moms tend to do), and I read the first paragraph of that article. I came to a sentence that made me stop in my tracks: "For the first time in two centuries, the current generation of children in America may have shorter life expectancies than their parents."

The article went on to explain that with rising rates of obesity and food-related illnesses, such as autoimmune disease, the problem would only get worse.

I reread that sentence and looked down at my perfect, healthy baby and the contrast hit me like a bolt of lightning. My mother lion instinct kicked in again and every cell in my body rebelled against that statement. At that moment, I decided that statistics like that weren't good enough for my child—or any child.

That moment ignited in me a passion for helping change those statistics and empowering other parents to do the same. I knew that if I could help parents understand that the power to make a change is in our hands, then together we could make a difference in the lives of our children—the lives of our entire family. After all, we are raising the future generation. We can teach them healthful habits and attitudes about food so that they aren't doomed to suffer the future those statistics predict.

Also, we control about 80 percent of the food budget and can vote with our dollars to change the food industry. If we decide to make a change, we will succeed because we care more about the future generation than anyone else. They aren't just statistics to us; they are our precious children.

Since that day a decade ago, I've been on a journey to improve the health of my family and to help other moms improve their family's health as well. My journey is now shared with my husband and six kids. Along the way, I've learned a little about parenting, a lot about cooking and cleaning, and so much about myself. I was diagnosed with Hashimoto's thyroiditis, which became a tremendous catalyst for personal change, as my lack of energy and health struggles were making it difficult to take care of my family. It took years for me to get answers, but I now know that my years of eating processed foods and living a high-stress lifestyle that lacked sleep created a prefect breeding ground for this autoimmune disease. A nourishing diet, however, is helping my body reverse these problems.

Through this struggle, I've realized how nourishing food is absolutely essential to health and how the standard diet is failing many of us! I began to research nutrition and the most healthful lifestyle—from what to eat to how to live overall—and I realized that with some basic changes in my diet and lifestyle I could make a large impact on my health and the health of my family. I became my own guinea pig, experimenting with real food, supplements, and lifestyle changes to try to find my own answers. I read hundreds of books, listened to dozens of podcasts, and found hundreds of medical studies that became the basis of the changes I made.

My journey started with simple changes. It started with addressing my own health struggles and establishing mindful eating and lifestyle habits for my family. Long before I was "Wellness Mama," I was just a new mom with a fussy baby and an undiagnosed thyroid problem struggling to figure out why my hair was falling out and my hands were always cold. I was a new wife, learning how to cook for my family and researching the chemicals in my cleaning products.

I started with baby steps, making one natural product for my home . . . then planning a couple real-food meals each week. I slowly replaced the plastic in our house with glass or steel items and stocked my pantry with organic ingredients. The journey started slowly but grew quickly and as I began to see how much healthier and happier my family was, I started sharing my remedies recipes with friends and family.

These changes and my passion for them grew into a blog and a website that allowed me to share my knowledge. The more I learned, the more I wrote, and the reaction from others was so great and so encouraging that I kept at it. Eventually it exploded as I reached more and more people who like me wanted to help their children and themselves.

During the process, I worked to overcome my own health struggles and to improve the health of my family at the same time. I'm not perfect. My family isn't perfect. I am very much a work in progress, but I think we all are. This book is part of my desire to share my own journey and what I've learned so that other families won't have to struggle with the same learning curve I did. The recipes and advice in this book, I hope, will make your life a little easier and your family much healthier.

You thought you were buying a cookbook, but my mission is to recruit you to change your future and the future of our children! In the book, not only will you find two hundred of my favorite healthful family-friendly recipes, but you'll also find some guidelines on what to eat and what to avoid as you begin your own journey. These guidelines are based on years of research, reading, and interviewing experts in the field of health and wellness. They bring together what I've learned during my own quest for wellness and reflect what I believe to be the healthiest way to eat and live. Once you are armed with that knowledge, I'll also share some of the best Tips for getting a simple, healthful meal to the table every night. After all, that's the key to improving your health and the health of your family. I hope you'll join me on this mission and that together we can make lasting changes.

Happy reading and happy cooking!

Warmly,
Katie
"the Wellness Mama"

the original wellness mama

"Do you work, or are you just a mom?" I can't even count the number of times that I've gotten that question over the years, often as I pushed a cart full of kids around the grocery store or at parties or events with other moms. Though the answer is technically "both," the question has always bothered me. After all, I do have a job that is beyond the scope of being a mother to my children. I have outside obligations that make income—my work as a writer and my job running the Wellness Mama website and online platform for moms. This job, though, is an extension of and inspired by my primary "work" as a mother.

Over time, I think that we, as women and mothers, have been fed a lie that being a mom is not enough and that we should also have an outside source of fulfillment and work to feel accomplished. My problem with this idea is not that I think there is anything wrong with being a working mom, as I am one myself, but that it devalues the tremendous amount of work and sacrifice that all moms do whether or not they work outside the home.

Having served in both of these roles at different points in the last decade—working mom and stay-at-home mom—I can attest that they both have their own challenges and struggles, but most important, they share a vital and often-forgotten power.

You see, while we've been so busy with the "mommy wars" and debating the merits of different decisions as moms, we've forgotten the distinct power of moms and how much ability we have to change the future of our own families and of the world as a whole.

It doesn't take a rocket scientist to notice that there are a lot of health problems in our world today. There are daily news reports of rising rates of disease and obesity. Most alarming, these rates are rising the most quickly in younger population groups and even children.

Certainly, there are many factors that contribute to these problems, but food plays a tremendous role. Our foods aren't what they once were and many of the foods we are told are healthful are actually making us sick. Foods are marketed for their convenience, ease of preparation, and low cost, but these foods come at a price and our children are the ones who will pay this price.

In our desire to "do it all" for our families, we have often turned to these convenience foods

It is health that is real wealth and not pieces of gold and silver.
—MAHATMA GANDHI

because they let us feel that we truly can get everything done with work, school for the kids, making food for our families and keeping the household running, but we've lost something in the process.

On a practical level, we've lost the age-old wisdom of food preparation that was once passed down through families and taught by mothers to their children. We've also lost something even more important: the understanding of our power as moms.

Margaret Mead once said, "Never doubt that a small group of thoughtful, committed citizens can change the world; indeed, it's the only thing that ever has." This statement is true, but it is most true when it comes to the vital work of moms. We have the power to teach our children healthful habits (when it comes to diet and to life in general) and this is incredibly important.

My goal in starting the Wellness Mama website, and now in writing this book, is to empower and inspire other families to take back the power we've always had but have recently forgotten: the power to influence the future of our own health, our children's health, and even our world through our dietary decisions and the foods we purchase. I believe in the power of change and my large and growing Wellness Mama community does, too.

This doesn't have to be a drastic or life-altering change or even one that takes a lot of time, money, or effort; it's a subtle shift to make real food and family time a priority in our own lives.

I know it isn't easy, but it is possible.

I have six kids (whom I homeschool), two cats, a dog, a job (or technically three), and enough laundry and dishes to keep a hotel staff busy, but our family eats a homemade real-food meal each night. Together. I say this not to toot my own horn but to show that if I can do it, anyone truly can.

This book is my road map to show you how to make healthful eating and living as a family possible while still fostering the other important and necessary areas of your life. Together, we will walk through stocking a real food kitchen, organizing recipes, and creating simple to follow meal plans that take the stress out of preparing real-food meals for your family—and, dare I say, make the process fun!

real foods rule

In the last decade of trying to find my own health answers and the best way to feed my family, I've been through the gamut of health ideas and dietary dogma. I've tried the Paleo Diet, the Specific Carbohydrate Diet, the Gut and Psychology Syndrome Diet, the Autoimmune Diet, and practically every other possible dietary variation out there. While some of them were an important step in my own health journey and may be an important step in yours, you won't find any of those terms in this book.

You see, real food and healthful living supersede a simple dietary system or dogma. The diets mentioned above may offer a step in your learning process, but essentially, they all just point to the importance of the same foundational idea of consuming real, whole food on a regular basis.

Many of these diets are helpful in that they focus on removing processed foods and incorporating more vegetables, but they may also omit foods that have a place in a healthful diet. To help accommodate the widest number of real-food dietary needs possible, the more than two hundred recipes in this book are grain-free, dairy optional, and nutrient dense.

Of course, quality sources of grains, dairy, or other foods can be added if they work well for your dietary needs, but they aren't necessary, and I've found that focusing on the core aspects of high-quality protein, lots of vegetables, and beneficial fats allows for nutrient-rich and uncomplicated recipes that work for every family.

While this book doesn't follow any particular food philosophy other than the simple idea of eating real food, there are several types of "foods" that, after years of reading and researching, I now avoid for my own family and I suggest you also read up on them and consider avoiding or limiting them for yours. I feel that these foods are more often expensive, less nutritious, and simply not necessary for a healthful diet. Among these are processed grains, refined oils, refined sweeteners, and processed meats. Studies have shown that these highly processed foods are not able to nourish the body like foods in their whole, natural state can. Highly processed oils can create inflammation in the body, while refined sugars can lead to insulin problems and hormone imbalance. Let's look at each of these a bit more closely so you can understand why you might want to eliminate or reduce them in your daily life. Let's start with grains.

GRAINS AND GLUTEN

Grains, inexpensive and readily available, are the cornerstone of diet for many people, and they can be healthful when consumed in whole form and are not processed or refined. Unfortunately, most grains we consume in modern times are highly processed, sprayed with various pesticides and herbicides, and have artificial nutrients added to make up for the ones lost through refining.

Grains also contain controversial phytic acid

(also called phytate), which is found in the bran of all grains as well as the outer coating of seeds and nuts. This is the form that plants and seeds store phosphorus in, but it may not be the most beneficial form for humans. It is often cited as a compound that can prevent the absorption of calcium, magnesium, iron, copper, and zinc. Despite this drawback, phytic acid is an antioxidant and it may protect the body from certain conditions like kidney stones and cancer. Like many things in life, the devil is in the details.

Phytic acid is present in all plants to some degree but is highest in grains and beans. When phytic acid binds to a mineral, it becomes a phytate, which is the energy source for a growing seed.

Historically, grains had to be processed by hand before they could be consumed. They were either stone ground or milled by hand. Often, they were left in the fields where a natural sprouting process would occur that reduced the phytic acid content.

The grains consumed today, however, are much more highly processed and finely ground than these historic grains, and we consume them in much larger amounts than people once did. Since the bran is often removed, phytic acid is not present in the amounts in which it occurs in nature, and research suggests that its absence may lead to imbalances when grains are consumed in large amounts. Highly processed grains are high in simple carbohydrates that affect insulin production in the body. Insulin production is an important process for storing nutrients and processing glucose in the bloodstream, but regularly consuming too many processed carbohydrates can tax the insulin system.

Let's take a trip back to freshman biology, shall we? When carbohydrates, regardless of their source, enter the body, they are eventually broken down into glucose. Any extra glucose floating around in the body that we are not immediately using is stored as fat by insulin. This is a natural response of our bodies, and it has allowed humans to survive for thousands of years, even through famine. If we aren't using the fuel now, our bodies store it for future use in the form of fat.

Fortunately for us, we are not commonly faced with famine, but because of this, we don't often get the chance to use up these excess fat stores, so the fat accumulates. If the carbohydrate consumption is excessive, the body throws in cortisol and adrenaline hormone production to handle the extra load. This whole hormonal song and dance does the tango on the body's endocrine and immune systems and creates inflammation in the body. When this happens regularly over a long period of time, it takes a very serious toll on the body.

Some people do just fine consuming unprocessed grains regularly, but a percentage of the population struggles with other compounds found in grains, including gluten and lectins.

Gluten is a sticky water-soluble protein that is found in many grains, including wheat, rye, and barley. Grains like corn, rice, and oats have similar proteins but do not contain gluten. In people with digestive or genetic issues that make them intolerant to these compounds, these proteins can cause problems by breaking down the microvilli in the small intestine over time.

Lectins are mild toxins that can inhibit the repair of the gastrointestinal track, especially in sensitive individuals. Lectins are not broken down in the digestive process and bind to receptors in the intestine, allowing them and other food particles to leech into the bloodstream. Nothing like predigested food circulating the bloodstream!

DO WE NEED GRAINS?

Some people can handle regular consumption of grains without a problem, but many sensitive individuals can't. To help make the real-food recipes in this book accessible to everyone, including those with sensitivities, autoimmune disease, and allergies, I have not included grains in these recipes and opted for substitutes (like coconut flour, vegetable noodles, etc.) that are higher in protein and vitamins. At our house, we often substitute nutrient-dense vegetables in place of processed grains whenever possible, and I've included our recipes that reflect this. But if you and your family tolerate grains well and want to add them to the recipes in this book, then go for it.

Unfortunately, especially when they are processed, grains do not have the nutritional profile that they often claim to have. It makes much more sense to get nutrients from foods like vegetables, fruits, proteins, and healthful fats, which offer much higher nutrient profiles without the drawbacks. In fact, dietary experts agree that most of us aren't consuming enough vegetables, and adding veggies to common family meals is an easy way to up consumption.

"But what about the fiber in grains?" some might ask. "And what about the vitamins and minerals?"

You know what else is a good source of fiber, vitamins, and minerals? Vegetables. You know which also has *more* fiber, vitamins, and minerals? Vegetables. And if you want to blow the nutrition profile of grains completely out of the water, try adding in foods like liver, homemade broth, fermented vegetables, and if tolerated, eggs.

THE TRUTH ABOUT NUTRIENTS IN GRAINS

Let's break down the reasons that we are often told that we need grains: fiber, vitamins, and minerals. Do grains really have spectacular amounts of these substances that are hard to find elsewhere?

FIBER

Fiber is often touted for its supposed ability to move things along in the digestive system. Researchers explain that high-fiber foods accomplish this when they puncture the cells of the gastrointestinal tract, which ruptures their outer covering and creates a layer of lubricating mucus to help heal the intestines.

We do need a certain amount of the right kind of fiber, but this fiber can be easily obtained from vegetables and fruit without the need for additional insoluble fiber from grains.

VITAMINS AND MINERALS

Much is made of the vitamin and mineral content in grains, specifically B vitamins and magnesium. As with fiber, these nutrients can be easily found in other foods, and, in fact, thiamin, riboflavin, folate, iron, and magnesium all appear in lower levels in grains than they are in vegetables. In other words, vegetables contain more vitamins and minerals per serving than grains do, without the potential for harm.

THE BOTTOM LINE

Grains do contain some nutrients, but these nutrients can be found in larger amounts in fruits, vegetables, and meats/fats. If your family does well with grains, by all means add them, but the recipes in this book are designed to help your family try a wide variety of vegetables and other nutrient-dense foods.

I agree with many nutritionists who say that going gluten-free isn't going to do much good if you just replace the gluten with gluten-free processed foods. These gluten-free processed alternatives often have more sugar and

chemical substances to balance out the lack of gluten.

If, however, you replace the gluten-containing foods (and all grains) with vegetables, fruits, fermented probiotic-rich foods, homemade broths, organ meats, and humanely raised animal meats, you will not be missing out on vitamins and minerals. In fact, according to the latest statistics I've seen for food consumption in the United States, you'll be head and shoulders above the rest of the population on vitamin and mineral intake.

Since grains are often fortified with additional nutrients, it is important to make sure that you are eating a varied diet rich in vitamins and minerals when you go grain-free.

Traditional cultures around the world where grains are consumed regularly or in large amounts have found ways to reduce the harmful components of grains, through methods like soaking, sprouting, and fermenting. These methods help change and preserve the nutrient content of grains so that they are more digestible to us. For example, soaking grains in a liquid acidic medium provides an ideal environment for them to sprout, and when grains are allowed to sprout, enzyme inhibitors are reduced or eliminated and nutrient absorption is enhanced. Similarly, a process like sourdough fermentation, which alters the chemical makeup of the grain, can both make the nutrients in grains much more bioavailable and reduce the antinutrient properties.

From a nutrient perspective, grains prepared in these traditional ways have much higher nutrient levels and lower levels of simple carbohydrates than what is found in refined and processed grains. For this reason, when consuming grains, I advise choosing soaked and sprouted varieties. These can be made at home, but you can also find presoaked and sprouted grains in stores as well.

Soaking, sprouting, and fermentation improve the nutrient profile of grains and make them easier to digest. If your family tolerates grains well, I'd suggest looking into these types of traditional preparation.

REFINED OILS

Refined vegetable oils are among the most misunderstood and overrecommended foods in the health community. You've probably heard these referred to as "heart-healthy oils," a good alternative to those "artery-clogging saturated fats."

These oils are supposed to help lower cholesterol and blood pressure, increase weight loss, and somehow improve overall health.

You won't find any refined seed oils in this cookbook though. Why? Let's take a closer look at vegetable oils and margarine.

Vegetable oils (and margarine, which is made from these oils) are oils extracted from seeds like the rapeseed (canola oil), soybean (soybean oil), corn, sunflower, safflower, and so on. The current form of these refined oils was nonexistent until the early 1900s, when new chemical processes allowed the oils to be extracted relatively easily; previously, only small amounts of cold-pressed oils from these seeds were available. Vegetable oils are now found in practically every processed food, from salad dressing to mayonnaise to conventional nuts and seeds, and today we consume them in much higher amounts than at any other time in history.

Unlike butter or coconut oil, vegetable oils can't be extracted in large amounts just by pressing or separating naturally. They must be chemically removed, deodorized, and altered. As a result, these oils are some of the most chemically altered foods in our diets.

HOW VEGETABLE OILS ARE MADE

Vegetable oils are created in a factory, usually from seeds that have been heavily treated with pesticides (soybeans are one of the most-sprayed crops).

Take, for instance, the common canola oil, the beauty queen of the vegetable oil industry. It is made from rapeseed but was given its cute 'n' cuddly name in the 1980s as part of a marketing report organized by a conference on monosaturates.

Rapeseed (and rapeseed oil) contains high amounts of erucic acid, which is harmful to the body, especially in large amounts, and which has been linked to heart problems. To help reduce the damage from the erucic acid, canola oil is made from an altered hybrid version of rapeseed called low erucic acid rapeseed.

The oil is produced by heating the rapeseed and processing it with a petroleum solvent to extract the oil. It is then heated again and acid is added to remove the nasty solids (wax) that occur during the initial processing phase. At this point, the newly created canola oil must be treated with more chemicals to improve its color and separate the different parts. In a final step, since all these chemical processes have given the oil a harsh smell, it is chemically deodorized to make it palatable.

If the canola oil is going to be made into shortening or margarine, it undergoes an additional process called hydrogenation to make it solid at cold temperatures. Unlike saturated fats (butter, coconut oil, etc.), vegetable oils are not naturally solid at cold temperatures and must be hydrogenated. It is during this process that those lovely trans fats we've heard so much about are created.

There's nothing like petroleum-produced, overheated, oxidized, and chemically deodorized salad dressing for dinner.

Compare this process to how olive oil is made. Step 1: Gather the olives. Step 2: Make the olives into a paste and sometimes add water. Step 3: Press or spin in a centrifuge to separate oils. A similar process is used on coconut oil and other natural oils.

Since vegetable oils are chemically produced, it's not really surprising that they contain harmful chemicals. Most vegetable oils and their products contain butylated hydroxyanisole and butylated hydroxytoluene, which are artificial antioxidants that help prevent food from oxidizing or spoiling too quickly. These chemicals have been shown to produce potential cancer-causing compounds in the body and have also been linked to liver and kidney damage, immune problems, infertility or sterility, high cholesterol, and behavioral problems in children. Vegetable oils also contain residues of the pesticides and chemicals used in their growth and manufacture and most often come from genetically modified sources.

VEGETABLE OIL IN EXCESS

Prior to the early twentieth century, most people got their fats from animal sources like meat, tallow, lard, butter, cream, and so on. The overall amount of fat consumed since then has not changed much (it has decreased slightly), but the type of fat has changed dramatically.

The consumption of vegetable oil didn't increase much until the 1950s, when a governmental campaign was launched to convince people to use vegetable oils and margarine and avoid "artery-clogging saturated fats." Today, people consume, on average, about seventy pounds of vegetable oils throughout the year. I wonder what seventy pounds of a "food" that was previously nonexistent in human consumption might do to our health. Add to this the fact that the animals we eat are also often fed genetically modified, pesticide-treated seeds and grains (instead of their natural foods, like grass) and the amount of omega-6 rich oils and seeds in our diet are really high!

But do these vegetable oils reduce the risk of disease, and do saturated fats increase it?

All one has to do is look at the statistics to know that it isn't true. Butter consumption in the early 1900s was eighteen pounds per person per year, and the use of vegetable oils almost nonexistent. Yet cancer and heart disease were rare. Today butter consumption hovers just above 4 pounds per person per year while vegetable oil consumption has soared—and cancer and heart disease are endemic.

There are many problems with vegetable oil consumption, and in my opinion, no amount is safe. To understand why, let's look at a few of the biggest problems with vegetable oils.

The fat content of the human body is about 97 percent saturated and monounsaturated fat, with only 3 percent polyunsaturated fats. Vegetable oils contain very high levels of polyunsaturated fats, and these oils have replaced many of the saturated fats in our diets since the 1950s.

The body needs fats for rebuilding cells and hormone production, but it has to use the building blocks we give it. When we give it a high concentration of polyunsaturated fats instead of the fats it needs, it has no choice but to incorporate these fats into our cells during cell repair and creation. The problem is that polyunsaturated fats are highly unstable and oxidize easily in the body. These oxidized fats can lead to inflammation and mutation in cells. This can lead to cancer and other potential health problems.

The body needs omega-3 and omega-6 fats, the two polyunsaturated fats, in balance, preferably a 1:1 ratio. Our modern diets, however, are often much higher in omega-6 fats, and this can lead to problems.

In one study, Dr. Vivienne Reeve, head of the Photobiology Research Group at the University of Sydney, irradiated a group of mice while feeding different groups of them polyunsaturated and saturated fats. She discovered that the mice that consumed only saturated fat were totally protected from skin cancer. Those in the polyunsaturated fat group quickly developed skin cancers. Later in the study, the mice in the saturated fat group were given polyunsaturated fats. Skin cancers quickly developed in those mice as well.

The 3 percent of our body that is made up of polyunsaturated fats is approximately half omega-3 fatty acids and half omega-6 fatty acids, and our body needs this balance. Omega-3s have been shown to reduce inflammation and be protective against cancer, while too much omega-6 fats cause inflammation and increase cancer risk.

Over time, consumption of oils high in omega-6s and polyunsaturated fats can also lead to other problems. In 1997, the journal *Epidemiology* published a study called "Margarine Intake and Subsequent Coronary Heart Disease in Men." The authors followed participants of the Framingham Heart Study for twenty years and recorded their incidence of heart attack. They also tracked both butter and margarine consumption.

The researchers discovered that as margarine consumption increased, heart attacks went up. As butter consumption increased, heart attacks declined.

The study divided the data into ten-year increments. What the authors discovered is that during the first ten years, there was little association between margarine consumption and heart attacks. However, during the second decade of follow-up, the group eating the most marga-rine had 77 percent more heart attacks than the group eating none! This suggests that perhaps the effect is cumulative, and while these refined oils may not cause a problem in the short term, they might create damage over time.

Imbalance of these fats can also cause dam-age to the intestines and, along with processed grain consumption, can set the body up for a host of food allergies and autoimmune prob-lems. (This was likely at least partially the cause of my own autoimmune disease.)

In light of all that information, how do you sort out which oils are healthful, and which ones aren't? Even more important, how do you know how much of each one to consume to be healthy?

OILS AND FATS TO AVOID

Our family avoids highly refined vegetable oils completely. There are more nutritious alterna-tives (which taste better, too!). Here are the main oils I avoid:

- Canola oil
- Corn oil
- Cottonseed oil
- Grapeseed oil
- Margarine
- Peanut oil
- Safflower oil
- Shortening
- Soybean oil
- Sunflower oil
- "Vegetable" oil
- Any other fake butter or vegetable oil products

While it is simple enough to avoid these oils themselves, the tougher challenge is avoiding all the foods they are in. Check out practically any processed food, and you will find at least one of these ingredients, often labeled as "par-tially hydrogenated corn/soybean/etcetera oil" or "May contain soybean or canola oil." These foods in particular often contain one of the above unhealthful oils:

- Artificial cheeses
- Chips
- Cookies
- Crackers
- Mayo
- Salad dressings
- Sauces
- Snack foods
- Store-bought condiments
- Store-bought nuts and snacks
- Practically anything sold in the middle aisles of the store

OILS AND FATS TO CONSUME

There are so many wonderful and healthful fats that are beneficial to the body, so there is no reason to consume the unhealthful ones above. Making the switch to the following healthier fats is a simple way to increase the nutritional con-tent of common recipes.

coconut oil. Filled with medium-chain fatty acids and lauric acid, coconut oil is an all-star of the saturated fats. Since the fat composition in cells in the body is largely saturated fat, it is important to get enough of it from healthful sources. Coco-nut oil does not oxidize easily at high tempera-tures or go rancid easily, making it a good choice for cooking and baking. It can be substituted for butter and also makes a great natural moisturizer.

butter. This is the one food people are happiest to start using again. Butter tastes delicious, and pastured, grass-fed butter is an excellent source of fat-soluble vitamins, healthful saturated fat, and other nutrients. It contains a compound that Dr. Weston A. Price, a dentist who studied many traditional cultures, called Activator X, known to improve nutrient absorption and have preventa-tive benefits against disease.

organic cream. Also a good source of healthful saturated fat, organic heavy cream is essentially liquid butter and is great served whipped on top of fruit, in desserts, or in cream-based recipes.

olive oil. High in monounsaturated fats (and low in polyunsaturated fats), olive oil is a great oil for salad dressings, homemade mayo, and cold recipes. It shouldn't be used for cooking since its high monounsaturated fat content makes it susceptible to oxidation at high temperatures.

palm oil. Has a high saturated fat content and is also heat stable. Some sources claim that palm oil production often encroaches on the natural habitat of some endangered animals, so we are careful to choose sustainably sourced palm oil. If in doubt, just use coconut oil.

avocados and avocado oil. A good source of monounsaturated fats and great on salads or in guacamole. Avocado oil is milky tasting and can be used in salad dressings.

fish. Fish are naturally high in omega-3 fatty acids and can help improve the omega-3/omega-6 balance in the body. Look for sustainable wild-caught sources, and stick to small fish like tuna, sardines, salmon, and so on to minimize mercury exposure.

eggs. Another all-star in the healthful fats community, eggs are loaded with vitamins, healthful fats, and necessary cholesterol. Consume them daily from free-range sources.

THE NOT-SO-SWEET TRUTH ABOUT SUGAR

Sugar exists in many forms besides just the white powdered (usually genetically modified) beet sugar we can pick up at the grocery store. Refined sugar affects the body in a powerful way and we are consuming more of it now than ever before. Every year, Americans spend over fifty billion dollars in dental bills, despite the fact that many of us have been told by a dentist to cut down or avoid sugar for the sake of our teeth.

In 1915, the average person consumed twenty pounds of sugar per year at most, while the USDA reported in 2014 that the average person consumes his or her body weight in sugar each year, excluding corn syrup and processed sweeteners. This means that a person of average weight (around 150 pounds) consumes 150 pounds of sugar and sweeteners per year!

This drastic change in sugar consumption in such a short period of time has created some not-so- sweet consequences.

I often hear the argument that sugar is okay in moderation and that eliminating any "food group" is dangerous. Certainly, avoiding an actual macronutrient category completely (carbohydrate, protein, or fat) could be problematic, but sugar itself is not a food group. Though sugar in some form is naturally present in many foods, by itself, it contains

- no nutrients
- no protein
- no healthful fats
- no enzymes

Really, sugar is just empty and quickly digested calories. Further, it can actually pull minerals from the body during digestion and create a hormone cascade that starts a positive feedback loop in the body to encourage more consumption. In a time when famine was common and we needed to consume large amounts of food in the summer while it was available in order to survive the winter scarcity, this was a good thing. In today's world of constant access to sugary foods, it is not.

Most often, when we talk about sugar, we are referring to a mixture of glucose and fructose, both simple sugars that are contained in various amounts in different foods. There are now dozens of sugar variations and artificial sweeteners in the standard diet today:

simple sugars (monosaccharides). These consist of dextrose, fructose, and glucose.

complex sugars (disaccharides). These are combinations of simple sugars like fructose and glucose.

sugar alcohols. Xylitol, glycerol, sorbitol, maltitol, mannitol, and erythritol are technically neither sugars nor alcohols but are becoming increasingly popular as sweeteners. They are not easily absorbed by the small intestine so they provide fewer calories than sugar but often cause problems with bloating, diarrhea, and flatulence.

sucralose. This Splenda ingredient is *not* a sugar. It is a chlorinated artificial sweetener similar to aspartame and saccharin, with detrimental health effects to match.

agave syrup. This processed sweetener is usually 80 percent fructose. The end product does not even remotely resemble the original agave plant.

honey. Consisting of about half fructose, it is completely natural in its raw form and has many health benefits—it contains as many antioxidants as spinach! It is best when used in moderation.

stevia. A highly sweet herb derived from the leaf of the South American stevia plant, in its natural plant form it is completely safe, though there may be some concerns with processed and bleached commercial versions that contain additives.

In my opinion, there is no safe amount of refined sugar since the body doesn't benefit from consuming it. Naturally contained sugars in fruit and vegetables are balanced by the fiber, vitamins, enzymes, and other properties, which slow sugar digestion and help the body deal with it more easily. Refined sugar, on the other hand, provides none of these benefits but instead many disadvantages, including these:

stresses the liver. When we consume fructose, it is digested through the liver. If liver glycogen is low, such as after exercise, the body will use the fructose to replenish liver glycogen. Most people, however, aren't consuming fructose only after a long workout and their livers are already full of glycogen. If fructose is consumed when the liver already has adequate glycogen and the body has an excess of fructose, the liver turns the fructose into fat to store it. Some of this fat is sent to the cells for storage, but some can remain in the liver. This is the condition referred to as nonalcoholic fatty liver disease.

increases bad cholesterol and triglycerides. This in turn increases the risk of heart disease.

can contribute to leptin resistance. Leptin functions like an appetite "thermostat." When leptin levels are low, food is perceived as highly rewarding; when leptin levels are high, food becomes less appealing. People with leptin resistance are not cued by their bodies to stop eating when their leptin levels increase, resulting in weight gain, cravings, sleep issues, and so on.

creates an addictive sugar response in the brain. When sugar is consumed, dopamine levels in the brain spike and reinforce the desire to consume more.

doesn't fill you up and instead encourages you to eat more. Sugar doesn't satiate the appetite and it can spike your blood sugar, leaving you hungrier than you were before you ate any.

EATING IN THE REAL WORLD

I realize that in today's world, it can be tough to completely avoid refined sugar since it is in practically everything. Unfortunately, the widespread availability of sugar doesn't make it any more healthful. Especially for kids who are still developing their nutritional foundation, metabolism, and hormones, even a little sugar can be harmful. As hard as it can be sometimes, my family tries to stick to whole, real foods as much as possible and avoid any processed foods (especially those containing grains and sugars). For us, this means cooking at home almost all the time. We work to teach our children about healthful eating, and we eat well when at home. I don't completely restrict unhealthful foods if we are away from home, though. My kids are young and so it is easy to make sure they are eating healthful foods, especially at home. One day, though, they will grow up and be away from home and exposed to all types of foods. I think it is important to let them start to make food choices on their own (and they usually make healthful ones) while they are still young and I can still help guide their choices rather than completely restrict them.

When kids are used to eating a really healthful diet, even a small amount of processed food will usually make them feel "yucky" and discourage them from eating it again. Exposure to other foods often leads to conversations about different types of foods and which are good and bad for the body.

Since they aren't restricted or expected to only consume chicken fingers or hamburgers when we aren't at home, my kids typically make good food choices on their own and have become rather adventurous eaters. For instance, my two-year-old loves broccoli, olives, sardines, and other healthful foods. My philosophy is to make the good foods readily available and make the unhealthful ones few and far between.

We also don't consume sugary drinks, not even juice. The only reason we keep sugar around is for making kombucha, water kefir, and homemade sodas. In these drinks, the majority of the sugar is fermented out and converted to beneficial bacteria before we drink it.

Our breakfasts usually consist of eggs or leftovers, lunches are salads or soups, and dinners are often baked or grilled meat with lots of veggies.

Sounds like a lot of work? It certainly is more work than a meal-in-a-box, but it is so worth it! We haven't had to take any of the kids to the doctor in years for illnesses, all but one have never had antibiotics, and they are happily active and fit naturally. My hope as they grow is to nurture their own healthful eating habits and develop a lifelong foundation for healthful eating.

making real food work for your family

Planning meals ahead of time and keeping a well-stocked kitchen are both essential for sticking to a real-food lifestyle. If you've got healthful foods at your fingertips all the time and no processed foods to fall back on, you won't be tempted to reach for the cereal on a busy morning or that boxed, frozen food for dinner. It took me a long time to learn the importance of being prepared. With a full-time job and a large family, organization is key. In this chapter, I share my secrets to having a pantry and refrigerator stocked with healthful foods at all times, so you can whip up a great stress-free meal or snack at a moment's notice.

People are always asking me how I am able to work, run a household, homeschool my kids, and still put three healthful, home-cooked meals on the table every day. The answer is: I'm a planner. And I want you to be, too, since I think it's key to living a healthful lifestyle. As my husband is so fond of saying to our children, "Proper prior planning prevents poor performance."

In this chapter, I will also share with you my Tips and advice for meal planning and cooking in order to make your life easier. Follow my advice (along with my recipes) and you'll spend less time cooking and preparing your meals and more time enjoying them with your family.

STOCKING A REAL-FOOD PANTRY

When you must keep large amounts of nonperishables on hand, buying them in bulk when they are on sale is a great way to save money. I have really limited pantry space, so instead of all my nonperishables being in one big closet, they are spread out all over my kitchen. Luckily, I cook with a lot of fresh or frozen ingredients, so they don't compete for space. These are the foods I keep in my pantry at all times:

coconut products. We go through coconut oil, shredded coconut, coconut flour, coconut cream, and so on quickly. In addition to being staples of many of my recipes, they make great snacks! Look for organic unrefined, cold-pressed versions.

olive oil. This is a great source of monounsaturated fats and perfect for making salad dressings and adding to foods once they are cooked. Just don't use it for cooking or it can oxidize!

Family is not an important thing. It's everything.
—MICHAEL J. FOX

other fats and oils. Lard, tallow, and ghee—I either make or order these in big quantities and store in one- or five-gallon buckets to keep on hand for cooking.

vinegars. I use white vinegar for cleaning and other vinegars, like balsamic and apple cider, for cooking. I also use apple cider/balsamic/red wine vinegars for salad dressings and marinades, and I drink a couple of tablespoons of apple cider vinegar in water if I feel a cold coming on.

nuts. Walnuts, cashews, almonds, macadamia nuts, and so on are great for on-the-go snacks. If I can, I soak and then dehydrate them before storing to reduce the phytic acid. (Macadamia nuts that have been dipped in 90 percent dark chocolate and then cooled are one of my favorite treats.)

canned fish. Though not the perfect choice, canned fish is a way to pack protein on the go or to make a fast meal in a pinch. I keep sardines, tuna, and wild-caught salmon on hand to make tuna salads, salmon patties, and so on. There are even organic sustainable tuna options.

self-canned veggies. I've been canning most of my own veggies and sauces to reduce our exposure to bisphenol A (BPA). Many store-bought canned vegetables, including all tomatoes (as far as I know), have a BPA lining in the can. It is certainly time consuming, but I make ketchup, tomato sauce, tomato paste, diced tomatoes, hot sauce, and tomato soup and more from the tomatoes in our garden. If you don't have this option, look for these foods in glass jars, not cans!

vegetables. Vegetables that don't need to be refrigerated can keep in the pantry for a long time. We keep sweet potatoes, onions, winter squash, and garlic on hand in the pantry, and they always get eaten before they spoil.

baking ingredients. My pantry always contains almond flour, baking powder (aluminum free), baking soda, cocoa powder, vanilla, almond butter, and dark baking chocolate.

dried herbs and ground spices. I have an entire cabinet stocked with nothing but medicinal and culinary herbs and spices. In my opinion, the right high-quality spices can make the difference between a good meal and a great one. I also use my herbs to make iced herbal teas, tinctures, and for medicinal use if one of us gets sick. For culinary uses, these are my staples:

- basil
- thyme
- oregano
- rosemary
- garlic (powder, granules, minced, salt)
- turmeric
- cayenne pepper
- cinnamon
- sea salt
- cumin

Also, check out my homemade spice blends in Sauces, Seasonings, and Spices and some homemade herbal tea recipes in Delightful Drinks.

STOCKING A REAL-FOOD FRIDGE

The fridge is harder to keep stocked, at least in my house. As fast as my kids go through eggs, bacon, apples, and cucumbers, it never seems to stay full! But these are the items I always try to keep stocked in my fridge:

vegetables. Sliced cucumbers, carrots, and celery are on hand for snacks. I also keep lots of lettuce and spinach for salads. Sauerkraut is usually in some stage of fermentation on my counter. To mix things up, I try to also keep artichokes, leeks, peppers, tomatoes, avocados, cauliflower, broccoli, greens, and squashes on hand.

fruits. We try to stick with seasonal fruit, but I keep apples and bananas around for the kids. If they are in season, we stock up on citrus fruits. If not, I keep lemon and lime juice for adding to water.

coconut milk. There is always at least a gallon of homemade or store-bought coconut milk in the fridge for smoothies and drinks for the kids.

yogurt. I keep a full-fat organic container on hand to separate into whey for fermenting.

meats. These are kept in the fridge or freezer and I usually don't keep more than one or two days' worth of meat defrosted at once.

condiments. I've resorted to making most of my own, but the following condiments are usually in the fridge: Honey Mustard (page 313), Homemade Mayonnaise (page 320), Homemade Ketchup (page 315), homemade marinara sauce (see page 319), Frances's Red Hot Sauce (page 323), apple cider vinegar, lemon juice, lime juice, and homemade pickles and relishes.

FREEZER AND BEYOND

To be able to purchase in bulk, we have a stand-up deep freezer and an extra fridge. We also keep a garden. The deep freezer is full of a quarter of a cow that we purchased from a local farmer and some frozen veggies from last year's garden. I also stock up on nitrite-free bacon, sausage, and hot dogs when they are on sale. During the summer, most of our vegetables come from the garden, which helps the food budget a lot!

BUYING ORGANIC

What our grandparents would have just called "food," we now refer to as "organic food" and often have to go to great lengths to source it. Sadly, food quality and nutrient levels have declined in recent decades, while pesticide and herbicide use has increased.

With over five hundred chemicals registered for use in agriculture in the United States (including many that have not been fully tested for safety), choosing organic food is one small way we can reduce unnecessary chemical exposure.

Choosing organic is especially important with animal products, as nine out of ten pesticides consumed are found in the fat of animal tissue. On an even larger scale, choosing organic foods protects our environment from chemical pollution as well and encourages sustainable farming practices.

For the best prices and most nutrients, try to find local organic options when possible from farmers' markets, CSAs (farms with community-supported agriculture), and local vendors.

ALWAYS BUY ORGANIC	SAFE TO BUY NONORGANIC
• Apples	• Asparagus
• Berries	• Avocado
• Celery	• Bananas
• Cherries	• Broccoli
• Cucumbers	• Cabbage
• Grapes	• Citrus fruits
• Kale	• Eggplant
• Lettuce	• Kiwi
• Peaches	• Mangoes
• Pears	• Onions
• Peppers	• Peas
• Potatoes	• Pineapple
• Spinach	• Sweet potatoes
• Summer squash	• Watermelon
• Tomatoes	

meal planning made easy

Meal planning is the most important factor when it comes to adopting and maintaining a real-food diet. It's easy to cook a quick convenience food or head to a restaurant when everyone is hungry and nothing is defrosted, but a little planning can prevent this afternoon conundrum! If you have kids, you can involve them in the planning as well, which will help them get excited about (and willing to try) the healthful foods you are cooking. Meal planning has literally changed our lives, reduced my stress, and made healthful eating not just doable but also easy. To keep things simple, I employ seven meal-planning methods.

1. USE A DAILY TEMPLATE EACH WEEK
Rather than starting from scratch each week, I have a template of the general types of foods I cook each day of the week and the number of times I use each main food. For example, each week for dinner I cook:

- 1 to 2 stir-fries
- 1 salad
- 1 slow cooker or soup meal
- 1 fish/seafood meal
- 1 to 2 prepare-ahead oven meals

I try to use no meat more than twice, so in a given week I might have two beef meals, two chicken meals, one fish meal, and two pork or egg meals.

2. FOCUS ON CORE RECIPES
As you find recipes your family enjoys, make them core recipes that get reused every few weeks. Try to build up about twenty of these and you won't ever be bored with your meals.

Each week, use these core meals for five of your dinners and try something new for two dinners. If you get really motivated, build twenty core meals for each season: Find favorite dishes that use seasonal produce and rotate with the seasons. This will also save money on produce.

3. STRETCH THE PROTEIN
Protein is typically the most expensive part of the meal, so if you can use less expensive cuts of meat and stretch them, it might allow you to

All great change in America begins at the dinner table.
—RONALD REAGAN

buy organic and grass-fed rather than conventional meats. This is another reason I love stir-fries and casseroles: You can add more veggies and stretch the meat more than if you were just serving baked chicken alone. The slow cooker is a great way to make tougher, cheaper cuts of meat tender.

4. MIX IT UP WITH SPICES

A basic easy recipe (like Beef & Cabbage Stir-Fry on page 151 or One-Pan Pakistani Kima on page 158) can taste completely different just by changing the spices. Add some cumin and chili powder and you have a Mexican-style dish or some curry for an Indian flavor. Basil, thyme, oregano, and garlic give an Italian flavor while Chinese five-spice lends an Asian flair. I buy all my herbs in bulk or grow them myself since it saves money and I'm able to use fresher and higher-quality herbs this way.

5. TRAVEL THE WORLD IN THE KITCHEN

One of my dreams is to travel the world and try the different cuisines in each country. Since that isn't possible right now, I try to create the same experience in my kitchen. With a little research and some healthful adjustments, you can re-create recipes from around the world. You might be surprised to find that your kids enjoy the flavors of Indian or Thai food or that you have a passion for French-style cuisine.

6. DON'T BE A SHORT-ORDER COOK

Want to raise picky eaters? Let your children eat whatever they want and cater to their food preferences. Want to raise children with a diverse palate and an enjoyment of real food? Expose them to healthful and diverse foods from a young age and don't make any specific foods for them. My one-year-old gladly eats curries, cooked vegetables, liver, and avocado because she's never had crackers, toast, processed chicken nuggets, or juice. Not only is this more nutritious for kids, but it will really be a benefit to them in the long run. Check out Overcoming Picky Eating (page 39).

7. EAT LEFTOVERS FOR BREAKFAST AND LUNCH

It can be tough to break the cereal-and-sandwich mind-set, but an easy time-saving way to eat healthfully is to make extra food for dinner and serve leftovers in a reimagined way for breakfast and lunch. Most foods (except soups) can also be added to an omelet for breakfast or put with a salad for lunch. Leftover meat wrapped in nori or coated in barbecue sauce, for example, makes a delicious breakfast or lunch.

Another easy trick is to use mason jars to make mealtime easier. Make mason-jar salads for easy breakfasts or lunches (liquid ingredients at the bottom for salads, then meat/toppings, then lettuce) and store them in the fridge. You can also store leftovers like soups and stir-fries in the jars so they can be reheated easily or dumped onto a plate to serve.

Also, check out the rotating "Two-Week School Lunch Meal Plan" (page 46) for ideas on kids' lunches.

TIME- AND MONEY-SAVING TIPS
PREPARE IN BULK

Now that meal planning is a regular part of our lives, I've been able to work in preparing some foods in bulk to save time on future meals. This can be done in two ways: by preparing double portions of a meal and freezing one or by preparing a large but inexpensive base ingredient (like a meat) that can be repurposed throughout the week for several meals.

When our budget is tightest, I prepare a large

inexpensive cut of meat and reuse it different ways throughout the week. I always keep an eye out for items like turkey, ham, or brisket to go on sale for these occasions.

Last year, for instance, I found whole turkeys on sale for thirty-nine cents a pound, which worked out to between five and six dollars per turkey. I bought seven! Now, when we have company (or even when we don't), I just stick a turkey in the oven and have leftovers for the whole week.

Here are some examples of how to make the most out of your leftover meats:

- **Turkey.** Leftover meat can be rolled in lettuce leaves for lunches, made into turkey enchiladas for dinners, placed in your slow cooker for soups, added to omelets, or put in stir-fries.
- **Beef.** Leftover meats, such as briskets and roasts, can be seasoned for fajitas, added to omelets, made into barbecue, thrown in soups, even made into omelet quesadillas.
- **Ham.** Leftover ham can be served with roasted cauliflower for a "ham and potatoes" dish, put in omelets, wrapped up in lettuce or chopped for a salad topping, or added to a stir-fry with cabbage.

To further stretch the budget, use the bones of any meat you eat to make a healthful bone broth or stock (see Bone Broth Tutorial with Five Variations on page 152). Broth can be stored in the freezer for up to two months or canned and kept up to a year (make sure you follow instructions carefully when using any kind of meat product).

USE INEXPENSIVE AND SEASONAL VEGETABLES

Veggies can vary tremendously in price, depending on the time of year and the source. Focusing on veggies that are in season will help reduce your food budget and also prioritizes vegetables when they are most nutrient dense.

In the winter, we use a lot of frozen vegetables since they are cheaper and, in my opinion, frequently fresher than the "fresh" produce that has been shipped halfway around the world.

Vegetables like cabbage and sweet potatoes are inexpensive year-round and can be great fillers and substitutes in recipes. I stock up on things like these when they are in season, usually buying several cases of sweet potatoes in the fall from farmers' markets. Cabbage costs just pennies a pound from farmers when in season and can be made into sauerkraut for later use. And winter squash also stores well and we buy this in bulk, too.

ORDER NONPERISHABLES IN BULK

Though there is an upfront cost, ordering in bulk can usually save money in the long run. We order nonperishables like coconut flour, shredded coconut, olive oil, coconut oil, herbal teas, almond flour, and other ingredients in bulk from a co-op.

We also order cheese in bulk ten- to twenty-pound blocks at a time from an organic farmer who offers raw cheese (and cut them into smaller blocks to store in the freezer). Finding these resources in your area can be tricky, but once you establish a relationship with farmers, it can be a tremendous help to the budget.

FIND A CSA, FARMERS' MARKET, OR LOCAL FARMER

Farmers' markets, CSAs, and local farmers are great resources for buying inexpensive veggies and meats in bulk.

Websites like LocalHarvest.com and EatWell Guide.com can help you find a farmer, CSA, or farmers' market in your area. Websites like EatWild.com have resources for finding a local supplier of grass-fed beef or other meats.

Ask around, too! We get most of our meats and vegetables from Amish farmers, but they don't have listings online. Check with local health food stores—many will know places to find these items locally.

GROW YOUR OWN FOOD

Even if you live in a big city, it is often possible to grow at least some of your own food. We have a 25 × 40–foot garden for vegetables and also have fruit trees, grapevines, and blueberry bushes in the works this year. We are able to grow enough vegetables for summer, with excess that we preserve throughout the year, for our family of eight in this space. We offset a lot of our food bill last year by growing our own, and it was much easier than I expected.

I haven't tried it myself, but a lot of people recommend square-foot gardening to maximize space in small yards. Consider checking out a book on this if you are tight on space.

PRESERVE WHEN POSSIBLE

Preserving foods in various ways helps extend the amount of time seasonal foods can be used and is also a great budget-friendly way to store food. Last year I tried my hand at canning, and we are still enjoying the outcome. In fact, I've found that it is easy to can tomato products, applesauce, and many condiments, and this has been a great way to save money and make sure we are avoiding unwanted additives in our foods.

Freezing is another way to preserve foods, and our extra freezer in our shed has been a tremendous help for storing beef purchased in bulk and veggies from the garden.

Dehydrating is another option, though it takes a while and can be a slow process, at least with my dehydrator. If money is tight, look for dehydrators and canners at garage sales and thrift stores rather than buying new.

DON'T BUY DRINKS

If you are trying to eat healthfully, hopefully you've already cut out things like soda, canned drinks, and processed juices from your food budget. If not, do it now! This alone is a big step in improving overall health.

If you have consumed much of these beverages in the past, go back and look at the percentage of your food bill that they take up. In general, buying beverages in any prepared form is an expensive and unhealthful option. Even fruit juices contain much more sugar than people often realize and are expensive without offering much nutrition. Cutting those items from the grocery budget will often free up a lot of cash for more healthful options.

SAVE MONEY ELSEWHERE

Organic and grass-fed food options can certainly be more expensive than processed and premade foods, but they don't have to be with the right amount of planning. For us, making high-quality foods a nonnegotiable budget item has helped us prioritize them and consume them without stress. There are other areas of a budget where you can save money to help buffer the food bill also.

do not make a habit of eating out. I admit it: I love eating out. Not because the food is good (it usually isn't) but because it means that I don't have to cook or clean for one whole meal. This is a big deal when you cook three hot meals a day and then have to do the dishes (and mop the floor as the case may be with a one-year-old!). That being said, eating out even once a month can use up a lot of the food budget. Eating out less often helps me provide more healthful options for my family at home—and none of us miss eating out that much.

make expensive baby items at home. I've saved money by making my own natural baby wipes, baby food, and cloth diapers. All of these items are expensive in stores and are more healthful when made at home.

make your own natural cosmetics/beauty products. Try using some natural homemade substitutes for conventional beauty products or making your own deodorant and toothpaste.

make your own cleaning products. This one is so easy and saves a lot of money. If you aren't doing this already, you should be, and you probably already have the stuff at home. White vinegar, baking soda, washing soda, and natural soap are often all you need to keep your home clean naturally and inexpensively.

cut back on supplements. Unless you are taking a supplement for a particular condition, chances are you can back off on some supplements when you start eating more mindfully. You can also get vitamins, minerals, and probiotics easily by making herbal teas, bone broths, and kefir/kombucha. If you have to cut back on the supplements to eat a real-food diet, consider it a fair trade. Supplements are meant to "supplement" a good diet anyway, and it's really impossible to out-supplement a bad diet. In general, it is better to have healthful food options than to pop pills.

exercise at home or with your kids. Chances are you already have running shoes (or not: the exercising barefoot trend is growing, and for good reason). If you are paying for a gym membership, consider using this money for real food instead. Go for a run or a bike ride, do some sprints outside, or learn how to do proper push-ups at home. Make exercise fun without going to the gym by playing a game of soccer with the kids. Added bonus: You are keeping your kids active, too!

do a media detox. If you've made the above changes and money is still tight, consider doing a media "detox" by cutting back on entertainment-related expenses. We cut out cable a couple years ago, and we don't even miss it. Face it, the news is usually depressing and it doesn't seem to be getting much better. Consider getting rid of the cable or a newspaper or magazine subscription to have money to concentrate in health-focused areas of your life. Our kids don't get video games either (oh, the horror!), and they don't care. They have this great entertainment system called the backyard!

overcoming picky eating
in kids and adults

RULE #1
there is no complaining about food.

RULE #2
food is not a reward.

RULE #3
eating is a family activity.

RULE #4
try, try again.

RULE #5
hunger is okay.

RULE #6
focus on nutrient-dense foods.

Many parents assume that kids won't eat or like certain foods, even if the children themselves have never complained: In other words, they assume the children are picky eaters from the start, without any evidence, and set their kids up for this self-fulfilling prophecy.

There is a perception that foods like chicken nuggets, sandwiches, and prepackaged kid-size snacks are the foods of choice for kids, and we (as parents) are hesitant to introduce foods that we fear they won't like. Unfortunately, by doing this we create the picky eaters we fear we already have.

The only real stumbling block is fear of failure.
In cooking you've got to have a what-the-hell attitude.
—JULIA CHILD

I've also found that the attitude we teach about food is as important as the food choices we offer. Whenever I've visited other countries, I've been struck by the difference in how children ask for, eat, and behave in food-related situations. While I certainly think that the types of foods we market to and prepare for our children need to change, I think it is also important to change the way our kids think about food as well.

To this end, I pulled some ideas from my mom's French background (after noticing that her family was naturally thin, not picky, and ate a wide variety of foods). We've incorporated these ideas with our own children, and the difference has been astounding.

At our house, these are loosely called our "Food Rules," though the name is slightly misleading. I think that while we certainly must have guidelines about how children act in food-related situations, these rules should be taught by example and practice rather than an iron fist (or a wooden spoon). In many cases, these rules serve as a reminder for me in my attitude when presenting new foods, even more so than for the kids.

RULE #1: THERE IS NO COMPLAINING ABOUT FOOD

In our house, children (and adults) are not allowed to complain about food. This doesn't mean that they are forced to eat at every meal, just that negative talk about food is not permitted.

Food is first for nourishment, not just for taste or appearance, and this is an important thing to teach children. Additionally, complaining about food is both rude to the cook and shows a closed-minded attitude.

Focusing on the positive and avoiding complaining about food has made a big difference for our kids.

how we handle it: No one is ever forced to eat if truly not hungry, but everyone must sit and participate in meal times with a positive attitude. Those who insist on a negative attitude are dismissed for bedtime. Especially with multiple kids, a negative mentality about a certain food spreads quickly and is hard to counteract, so it is better to head this off promptly!

RULE #2: FOOD IS NOT A REWARD

Food is, again, first provided for nourishment, not entertainment or emotional reward. For this reason, we try (not always perfectly) not to bribe with food or offer food as rewards for good behavior. I even try not to make certain foods a big deal on birthdays or other occasions, as we try to focus on experiences instead. For example, instead of a birthday cake and sugary snacks, we might take a family trip to the zoo or other fun place for a birthday.

Nor do I ever present foods as a punishment or associate them with punishment. While children can't complain about food, it is the negative attitude that is disciplined, not the action relating to food.

I've seen in many children (and even to some degree in myself at times) an emotional connection to a certain food or a desire to eat certain foods in emotional situations. While the types of foods we provide are certainly important, it is also crucial to avoid creating an association between foods (especially unhealthful ones) and happy times or fond memories. I'd personally much rather those fond memories be connected to family time and experiences anyway!

how we handle it: While we do, of course, sometimes have treats, they are just given when I make them. We don't use them as a bribe, kids

don't "earn" them through good behavior or good grades, and we don't withhold them if children misbehave.

RULE #3: EATING IS A FAMILY ACTIVITY

I think that the trend of eating on the go and in isolation (while watching TV or doing something else) has contributed a lot to the negative attitudes children have about food. For this reason, we make a sincere effort to eat meals (especially breakfast and dinner) as a family when at all possible and to make this an enjoyable time.

The advantages are that mealtimes (hopefully) provide an enjoyable time for conversation and bonding with the children, which also facilitates slower and more mindful eating. In our house, the whole family also eats the same thing at each meal. Children don't get special kid-friendly foods and as soon as little ones can eat solids, they get tiny pieces of what the rest of us are eating. The family atmosphere helps encourage children to eat what is served and helps us parents avoid food battles.

If a food is unusual or a new food for us, we don't make a big deal about it and just present it to the kids with a positive attitude and assume that they will eat it. I've seen my husband choke down liver with a poker face (poor guy!) and the kids eat it readily because they have no idea that they shouldn't like it.

how we handle it: Mealtime is family time and outside activities are rarely allowed to interfere. Everyone eats the same thing and is expected to eat it with a positive attitude. We don't often snack, so everyone is ready to eat at mealtimes (though children do occasionally get healthful snacks if there will be longer than normal times between meals).

RULE #4: TRY, TRY AGAIN

To facilitate a nonpicky palate in kids, they get one small bite of each food being served at a given meal (one green bean, one bite of sweet potatoes, and a piece of chicken). When they finish one bite of each, they can request more of any food. When children don't like a food or request it when asking for more, we just explain that it is okay as long as they are always willing to try it and explain that one day (when they are grown up) they will like the food.

Dislike of foods is not set in stone, so we don't force-feed huge amounts of foods that they don't necessarily like. We just set the expectation that they will keep trying those foods until they do.

how we handle it: Just as negative comments about food are not allowed, we try to promote a positive attitude about new foods by presenting them in manageable (one bite) amounts accompanied by the expectation that they will learn to enjoy all foods one day.

RULE #5: HUNGER IS OKAY

I know people who have completely lost a natural sense of hunger due to constant access to foods and eating on the go. It is perfectly normal (and expected) to be hungry before mealtimes and hunger is never an excuse for negative attitudes about food or eating junk food.

Normal hunger at mealtimes encourages kids to eat what is served and to eat enough to avoid being hungry too far in advance of the next meal. At the same time, a child who complains and is excused from the dinner table for bedtime quickly learns to have a more positive attitude (it has never taken one of our kids more than two nights total of missing family dinner to find an improved attitude).

how we handle it: We don't let hunger be an excuse for unhealthful eating or bad attitudes. We don't often offer snacks because children who are at least slightly hungry tend to be happier and more adventurous eaters at mealtimes.

RULE #6: FOCUS ON NUTRIENT-DENSE FOODS

Now for a few details on the actual types of foods we eat and why. I noticed that my mom (and the French in general) spend more time eating a smaller amount of high-quality food. They enjoy it more and obsess about it less. To help make all of the above "rules" easier to implement, I focus on cooking nutrient-dense, rich foods from scratch each day. We incorporate bone broth, homemade pâté, raw cheeses, homemade sauces (that contain butter or cream), eggs, and egg-based foods like hollandaise sauce on a daily basis.

Not only are homemade omelets filled with veggies and topped with hollandaise delicious, but we are all more nourished and have received a boost of beneficial fats (as opposed to what we would get from a bowl of cereal). When possible, we let the kids help shop for or prepare the meals and I always make an effort to explain why certain types of food are more nutrient dense than others and how they benefit the body.

how we handle it: I cook from scratch every day, which is more time consuming than throwing a sandwich together, but it is worth it to me to help my kids learn a healthful attitude toward food.

get started meal planning

As I mentioned, planning is the single most important factor for adopting and sticking to a healthier lifestyle. Planning also helps reduce stress and is the most efficient way to shop and cook. Not only does it help avoid the 5 p.m. panic of trying to figure out what to make for dinner, but it allows you to premake parts of the meals for each week to save time on busy nights.

With a solid meal-planning routine, most families are able to shop only once a week, make some meals ahead of time on a less busy day, and save several hours a week of food preparation time. As an added benefit, spending twenty minutes meal planning each week can save up to 20 percent of a family's grocery budget since only what is needed is purchased.

I have designed a two-week family meal-planning and shopping guide to help you begin your journey toward eating well. I've also included a two-week school lunch menu to help with feeding the kids well while they are away from home. Of course, this could also be used as a guide for work lunches or when simply looking for meals on the go.

TWO-WEEK FAMILY MEAL PLAN: BREAKFAST + DINNER

WEEK 1

SUNDAY
- Simple Sausage Balls (page 70)
- One-Pan Pakistani Kima (page 158)

MONDAY
- Smoked Salmon & Cream Cheese Frittata (page 66)
- Chicken Satay Skewers (page 161), Satay Dipping Sauce (page 317), Sesame-Citrus Bok Choy Salad (page 114)

TUESDAY
- Berry-Chia Breakfast Crisp (page 82)
- Ginger-Orange Glazed Roast (page 197) and Creamy Cucumber-Dill Salad (page 93)

WEDNESDAY
- Apple-Cinnamon Muffins with Coconut Flour (page 53)
- Meatball-Stuffed Spaghetti Squash (page 162)

THURSDAY
- West Texas Omelet (page 69)
- Chicken Diane (page 170) and Butter-Baked Acorn Squash (page 92)

FRIDAY
- Coconut Protein Bars (page 59) and Orange Julius Smoothie (page 76)
- Savory Seafood Bisque (page 175) and No-Bake Meyer Lemon Bars (page 269)

SATURDAY
- Make-Ahead Kitchen Sink Breakfast Bowls (page 74)
- Greek Grilled Chicken with Tzatziki Sauce (page 145) and My Big Fat Greek Salad (page 116)

EXTRAS
- Chocolate-Cherry Bark with Coconut Oil (page 264)

WEEK 2

SUNDAY
- Sausage Sweet Potato Hash with Brussels Sprouts (page 73)
- Teriyaki Chicken Thighs (page 202)

MONDAY
- Spinach, Feta & Onion Frittata (page 67)
- Stuffed Sweet Potatoes (page 127)

TUESDAY
- Orange-Cranberry Almond Flour Muffins (page 54)
- BBQ Bacon-Apple Chicken (page 211) and Roasted Sweet Potato Salad (page 110)

WEDNESDAY
- Ten-Minute Blender Banana Waffles (page 75)
- Meat Loaf Cupcakes (page 130)

THURSDAY
- Angel Food Cake Smoothie (page 79)
- Chicken Caesar Salad (page 103)

FRIDAY
- Gorilla Green Smoothie (page 78)
- Simple Salmon Chowder (page 173)

SATURDAY
- Sweet Potato–Crusted Quiche Lorraine (page 63)
- Pork Carnitas (page 201) with Grapefruit & Avocado Salad (page 95)

EXTRAS
- Chewy Chocolate Chip Cookies (page 252)
- Baked Cinnamon-Chia Apples (page 266)
- Simple Chia Seed Pudding (page 263)

WEEK 1

MONDAY

- Chipotle Chicken Fingers (page 217) with Honey Mustard (page 313)
- Sliced cucumbers and carrots
- Gorgeous Grape Gell-O (page 85)
- Mocha Protein Smoothie (page 80)

TUESDAY

- Athena's Greek Meatballs (page 218)
- Tzatziki Sauce (page 325) and cucumber slices
- Kiwi slices and trail mix
- Angel Food Cake Smoothie (page 79)

WEDNESDAY

- Grain-Free Garlic-Herb Crackers (page 219) with cheese and ham slices
- Celery with almond butter and raisins
- Orange slices and walnuts
- Simple Chia Seed Pudding (page 263)

THURSDAY

- Lettuce tacos with meat, salsa, and avocado
- Red pepper slices and Not-So-Plain Plantain Chips (page 226)
- Blueberries and banana
- Homemade Yogurt (page 84)

FRIDAY

- Ham & Egg Breakfast Cups (page 65)
- Olives and cucumber slices
- Apple with yogurt dip and nuts
- Chia Seed Energy Gel (page 58)

WEEK 2

MONDAY

- Turkey-Avocado Temaki (page 225)
- Broccoli and homemade ranch dressing (see page 299)
- Melon pieces and Not-So-Plain Plantain Chips (page 226)
- Berry Powerful Smoothie (page 77)

TUESDAY

- Ground Beef Jerky slices (see page 215)
- Avocado slices and strawberries
- Almonds and Gorgeous Grape Gell-O (page 85)
- Orange Julius Smoothie (page 76)

WEDNESDAY

- Cranberry-Pecan Chicken Salad Wraps (page 234)
- Homemade sweet potato chips (see page 223) and cucumber slices
- Apples with almond butter and raisins
- Peaches & Cream Smoothie (page 81)

THURSDAY

- Halibut with Lemon-Butter Sauce (page 168) and Homemade Ketchup (page 315)
- Restaurant-Style Tartar Sauce (page 306) and pickle spears
- Grapes and pistachios
- Mocha Protein Smoothie (page 80)

FRIDAY

- Cold Dairy-Free Upside-Down Pizza (page 147)
- Steakhouse Chop Salad (page 100) with homemade ranch dressing (see page 299)
- Coconut Protein Bars (page 59)
- Gorilla Green Smoothie (page 78)

Family Meal Plan Shopping List

PRODUCE

- acorn squash 1½
- apple 1
- bok choy 1 pound
- blueberries ½ cup
- carrots 2
- celery 1 stalk
- chives, fresh, 2 tablespoons, chopped
- cucumbers 5
- dill, fresh, 1 bunch
- garlic 1 head, minced
- ginger ¼ pound
- green beans 1 pound
- green pepper 1
- lemons 6
- lime juice 1
- limes 3

- Meyer lemons 2¼
- onions 5
- oranges 7
- parsley, fresh, 1 bunch
- red bell peppers 1½
- red onions 3
- romaine lettuce 3 heads
- shallot 1
- spaghetti squash 2
- spinach, fresh, 4 ounces
- sweet potatoes 4 pounds
- thyme, fresh, ½ teaspoon, chopped
- tomatoes 3

MEAT AND SEAFOOD

- chicken breasts 4 pounds
- chicken broth 2½ cups
- chuck roast 4 pounds
- clams 2 6.5-ounce cans
- crabmeat 1 cup
- ground beef 2 pounds
- lobster 2
- sausage, ground, 2 pounds
- smoked salmon 5½ ounces

SWEETENERS AND BAKING SUPPLIES

- baking soda 1 teaspoon
- cocoa powder ¾ cup
- coconut sugar 1½ tablespoons
- dried cherries ½ cup
- gelatin powder ¾ tablespoon
- collagen powder 2+ tablespoons
- honey 1 cup
- maple syrup 1½ cups
- Medjool dates 6
- sugar ½ cup
- vanilla 4+ teaspoons

CANNED AND JARRED GOODS

- almond butter ½ cup
- applesauce 1 cup
- coconut aminos 5 tablespoons
- diced tomatoes 1 15-ounce can
- Dijon mustard 1 tablespoon
- Frances's Red Hot Sauce (page 323) or store-bought 2 teaspoons
- Kalamata olives ½ pound
- lemon 1
- Easy Marinara Sauce from Fresh Tomatoes (page 319) or store-bought 2 cups
- orange marmalade 1 cup
- SunButter or peanut butter ¼ cup

DELI AND PREPARED FOODS

- ham ½ cup diced
- pecans 2¼ cups
- salsa 1 cup

BULK FOODS

- chia seeds ¾ cup
- coconut flakes, unsweetened, 1¼ cups
- raisins ¼ cup
- sesame seeds 1 tablespoon
- sunflower seeds ½ cup

EGGS AND DAIRY

- unsalted butter 8 tablespoons (1 stick)
- Cheddar cheese, grated, 1½ cups
- Cheddar cheese 10 ounces
- cream cheese 5½ ounces
- large eggs 3 dozen
- feta cheese, crumbled, ½ cup
- Greek yogurt 2 cups

- heavy cream 2½ cups
- milk of choice 2 cups
- mozzarella cheese, grated, 1 cup
- Parmesan cheese, grated, ½ cup
- sour cream ½ cup

FLOURS, OILS, AND VINEGARS

- almond flour 4¾ cups
- coconut flour ¾ cup
- apple cider vinegar
- coconut oil
- olive oil
- red wine vinegar
- rice vinegar
- toasted sesame oil 1 teaspoon
- dry white wine ¼ cup

FROZEN FOODS

- berries 4¼ cups
- Asian-style vegetables 3 bags
- fish sauce 3 tablespoons
- rice wine vinegar ¼ cup
- wheat-free soy sauce 2 tablespoons

SPICES TO HAVE ON HAND

- black pepper
- curry powder
- dried dill
- dried oregano
- garlic powder
- ground cloves
- ground ginger
- ground turmeric
- Italian seasoning
- paprika
- salt of choice (Himalayan or Celtic preferred)
- white pepper

PRODUCE

- [ ] apples 6¼
- [ ] baby spinach 1 pound
- [ ] bananas 5
- [ ] Brussels sprouts ½ pound
- [ ] cauliflower 1 head
- [ ] celery 3 stalks
- [ ] cranberries, dried, ½ cup
- [ ] dill 1 bunch
- [ ] garlic 1 head
- [ ] ginger, fresh, 1-inch piece
- [ ] green onions 1 bunch
- [ ] lime 1 (for juice)
- [ ] onions 8
- [ ] oranges 4¾
- [ ] pineapple 1 15-ounce can
- [ ] pineapple, frozen, 1 cup
- [ ] pecans ¾ cup
- [ ] romaine lettuce 2 heads
- [ ] shallot 1
- [ ] spinach 1 bunch
- [ ] strawberries, fresh, 2 cups
- [ ] sweet potatoes 18 medium

MEAT AND SEAFOOD

- [ ] bacon 12 slices
- [ ] chicken breasts 3 pounds
- [ ] chicken broth 4 cups
- [ ] chicken thighs 2 pounds
- [ ] ground beef 2 pounds
- [ ] ground pork sausage
  2 pounds
- [ ] ham ¼ pound, diced,
  precooked
- [ ] pork roast 5 pounds
- [ ] salmon 1 15-ounce can

SWEETENERS AND BAKING SUPPLIES

- [ ] baking powder ½ teaspoon
- [ ] baking soda 1 teaspoon
- [ ] coconut sugar ½ cup
- [ ] dark chocolate chips 1 cup

- [ ] collagen powder 2 tablespoons (optional)
- [ ] honey 7 tablespoons
- [ ] maple syrup 1 cup
- [ ] sugar ½ cup
- [ ] vanilla 1 tablespoon
- [ ] vanilla extract 2 tablespoons

CANNED AND JARRED GOODS

- [ ] BBQ Sauce (page 326) or
  store-bought 1 cup
- [ ] coconut aminos ½ cup
- [ ] full-fat coconut milk 5 cups
- [ ] lemon juice 1 tablespoon
- [ ] Homemade Mayonnaise
  (page 320) or store-bought
  ½ cup

BULK FOODS

- [ ] chia seeds 1¼ cups
- [ ] sesame seeds 2 tablespoons

EGGS AND DAIRY

- [ ] Cheddar cheese, shredded,
  1 cup
- [ ] large eggs 2½ dozen
- [ ] feta cheese, crumbled,
  ½ cup
- [ ] heavy cream 2 cups
- [ ] milk of choice 4 cups
- [ ] Parmesan cheese, grated,
  1 cup
- [ ] sharp Cheddar cheese 1 cup
- [ ] sour cream 1 16-ounce
  container

FLOURS, OILS, AND VINEGARS

- [ ] almond flour 4½ cups
- [ ] coconut flour ½ cup
- [ ] coconut oil 1 cup
- [ ] olive oil ½ cup
- [ ] rice wine vinegar ¼ cup
- [ ] white wine vinegar ¼ cup
- [ ] Worcestershire sauce
  2 tablespoons

SPICES TO HAVE ON HAND

- [ ] black pepper
- [ ] chili powder
- [ ] coarse sea salt
- [ ] dried basil
- [ ] dried sage
- [ ] dried thyme
- [ ] dry mustard
- [ ] garlic powder
- [ ] ground cinnamon
- [ ] ground cumin
- [ ] salt of choice
- [ ] white pepper

breakfast

All happiness depends on a leisurely breakfast.

—JOHN GUNTHER

apple-cinnamon muffins
with coconut flour

TOTAL TIME 40 min. | **ACTIVE TIME** 15 min. | **MAKES** 12 muffins

Muffins are a classic breakfast food, but many recipes include as much sugar as a cupcake! These apple-cinnamon muffins are a nutrient-dense take on regular muffins with protein-packed coconut flour and extra eggs. A favorite at our house when served alone or alongside eggs or quiche.

5 large eggs

1 cup applesauce (no sugar added)

½ cup coconut flour

¼ cup coconut oil

3 tablespoons ground cinnamon

1 teaspoon baking soda

1 teaspoon vanilla extract (optional)

2 tablespoons honey (optional)

Preheat the oven to 400°F. Grease the cups of a muffin pan with oil and set aside.

Place the eggs, applesauce, flour, oil, cinnamon, baking soda, and, if using, vanilla in a medium bowl and use an immersion blender or a whisk to mix well. Let sit for 5 minutes, then spoon ⅓ cup of the batter into each muffin cup.

Bake for 12 to 15 minutes, until starting to brown and not soft when lightly touched on the top.

Let cool for 2 minutes, then drizzle with honey, if desired, and serve. Leftovers can be stored in the refrigerator in an airtight container for up to 1 week and reheated to eat.

orange-cranberry
almond flour muffins

TOTAL TIME 30 min. | **ACTIVE TIME** 10 min. | **MAKES** 6 muffins

These fragrant muffins add orange zest and juice and sweet cranberries to high-protein almond flour for a filling and delicious breakfast on the go.

2¼ cups almond flour

½ teaspoon baking powder

½ teaspoon salt

Zest and juice of 1 organic orange

3 eggs

¼ cup pure maple syrup

¼ cup coconut oil

½ cup finely chopped dried cranberries

Preheat the oven to 350°F. Line the cups of a muffin pan with paper or silicone liners and set aside.

Combine the flour, baking powder, and salt in a medium bowl and stir to combine. Zest the orange directly into the bowl with the dry ingredients, then add the orange juice, eggs, maple syrup, and oil and mix until well combined. Stir in the dried cranberries. Pour the batter into the muffin cups, filling each three-quarters full.

Bake for 20 to 23 minutes, until the center is set and the top has a golden brown color. Remove and let cool for 10 minutes before serving. Store in an airtight container at room temperature for up to 3 days.

coconut flour biscuits

TOTAL TIME 20 min. | **ACTIVE TIME** 5 min. | **MAKES** 8 biscuits

Biscuits are a common breakfast food for their versatility and ability to turn foods like eggs and bacon into finger foods. These simple-to-make coconut flour biscuits provide extra protein to give your day a jump start. A favorite at our house in eggs Benedict.

½ cup coconut flour

5 tablespoons coconut oil or melted unsalted butter

4 large eggs

2 tablespoons honey (optional)

½ teaspoon sea salt

½ teaspoon baking powder

Preheat the oven to 400°F.

Place the flour, oil, eggs, honey, salt, and baking powder in a medium bowl and mix with an immersion blender or a hand mixer until well incorporated. Using your hands, carefully form the batter into eight small balls and mash each one down with a spoon to make it about ½ inch thick.

Place the balls on a greased baking sheet. Then bake for 12 to 15 minutes, until just starting to brown.

chai coconut granola

TOTAL TIME 25 min.	ACTIVE TIME 5 min.	SERVINGS 8

Cereal is a favorite breakfast food for kids, but we avoid the boxed variety because it is more expensive and less nutritious. This homemade granola uses nuts, seeds, dried fruit, and unsweetened coconut flakes for a nourishing and delicious breakfast with a subtle chai flavor. Try serving it with Coconut Milk (page 278) or Almond Milk (page 278).

¼ cup coconut oil

¼ cup pure maple syrup or honey

1 teaspoon vanilla extract (optional)

2 cups unsweetened coconut flakes

½ cup nuts, such as cashews, pecans, or your choice

½ cup seeds, such as sunflower, pumpkin, or your choice

½ cup dried fruit, such as blueberries, cranberries, or your choice (optional)

1 tablespoon ground cinnamon

½ teaspoon ground nutmeg

½ teaspoon ground ginger

Preheat the oven to 350°F. Line a baking dish with parchment paper and set aside.

To a small saucepan, on medium heat, add the coconut oil, maple syrup, and, if using, the vanilla and let simmer for 5 minutes.

In a large bowl, mix together the coconut flakes, nuts, seeds, fruit, if using, cinnamon, nutmeg, and ginger. Pour the oil–maple syrup mixture over the dry ingredients and mix well. If the dry ingredients are not lightly coated, then add a little more oil and maple syrup in equal parts.

Spread out the granola on the prepared baking dish. Bake for 15 to 20 minutes, until starting to brown. Remove and let cool, then crumble the granola into pieces. Store in an airtight jar in the pantry for up to 2 weeks.

chia seed energy gel

TOTAL TIME 8 hr.　　**ACTIVE TIME** 10 min.　　**SERVINGS** 4

Chia seeds are nutrient powerhouses packed with omega-3s, calcium, and protein. When rehydrated and added to juice, they make a nutrient-dense chia gel.

1 cup filtered water

2 cups pomegranate, tart cherry, or any other unsweetened juice

Juice of 1 lemon

¼ cup chia seeds

Honey or sweetener of choice to taste (optional)

Mix all the ingredients in a pitcher or mason jar. Refrigerate overnight so that the chia seeds can hydrate and create a natural gel. Serve in bowls or cups and enjoy!

coconut protein bars

TOTAL TIME 2 hr. 10 min.   **ACTIVE TIME** 10 min.   **MAKES** 8 medium-size bars

Protein bars have firmly secured their place in our culture as a "healthful" meal replacement or snack, but many of them have as much sugar as a candy bar! They can also be pricy and are not a budget-friendly alternative for those of us with kids. Make your own with real-food ingredients to save money and sneak in some extra nutrients!

6 large Medjool dates

2 tablespoons melted coconut oil

½ cup almond or other nut butter

¼ cup honey (optional)

1 cup unsweetened shredded coconut, plus more to thicken if needed

½ cup chopped pecans or other nuts

¼ cup chia seeds

½ teaspoon ground cinnamon

Remove the pits from the dates and discard. Pulse the dates in a food processor with the oil until a paste forms. Add the almond butter and pulse for 1 minute, until combined. Scrape the mixture into a medium bowl and mix in the honey, if using, coconut, pecans, chia seeds, and cinnamon by hand to incorporate. Add more coconut and nuts if needed to thicken so that it is a spreadable paste consistency.

Line an 8 × 8-inch baking dish with parchment paper. Spread the mixture into the prepared dish and press into the sides. Refrigerate for 2 hours to harden. Remove and cut into 1 × 4-inch bars and serve immediately. Store in an airtight container in the refrigerator for up to 2 weeks or freeze for up to 2 months.

ham, gouda & leek
crustless quiche

TOTAL TIME 50 min.	**ACTIVE TIME** 10 min.	**SERVINGS** 6

Quiche is a classic breakfast food with endless variations. This is one of our family's favorites with leek, ham, and Gouda. You might be surprised to find that your kids love these "grown-up" flavors in this simple quiche.

2 tablespoons (¼) stick unsalted butter

1 medium leek

¼ pound baked ham, diced

12 eggs

½ cup heavy cream

1 teaspoon salt

1 teaspoon freshly ground black pepper

½ teaspoon dry mustard

6 ounces smoked Gouda cheese

Preheat the oven to 375°F.

Melt the butter in a medium skillet over medium-high heat.

Remove the outer layer of the leek and trim off the root and the tough parts of the green stems. Wash well, then thinly slice and dice and add to the skillet. Sauté for 5 to 10 minutes, until tender and the moisture has evaporated.

Add the diced ham and turn off the heat. Let cool while the flavors incorporate.

In a blender on medium speed, mix the eggs, cream, salt, pepper, and mustard powder.

Spoon the ham-and-leek mixture into a 9 × 13-inch pan and spread. This will also grease the pan. Slice the cheese and add to the pan. Pour the egg mixture over the ham and leek mixture. Bake for 35 to 40 minutes, until the center is just set. Remove, cool for 10 minutes, and serve. Store leftovers in the refrigerator for up to 3 days and reheat before serving.

sweet potato–crusted quiche lorraine

TOTAL TIME 90 min. | **ACTIVE TIME** 15 min. | **SERVINGS** 6

I adore this rustic quiche recipe, which uses sliced sweet potatoes in place of a crust for extra flavor and nutrition. The crust can be used with any quiche recipe, but I love it in this classic quiche Lorraine! Using any vegetable in place of a refined flour crust is a great way to increase flavor and nutrition.

2 tablespoons coconut oil to thickly grease pan

1 large sweet potato

¼ pound baked ham or cooked bacon

1 cup grated Cheddar cheese

1 shallot

8 large eggs

½ teaspoon salt

½ teaspoon freshly ground black pepper

½ teaspoon garlic powder

½ teaspoon dry mustard

2 cups heavy cream or 1 cup Coconut Milk (page 278)

Preheat the oven to 375°F. Grease a 9 × 13-inch baking dish with coconut oil and set aside.

Peel and thinly slice the sweet potato using a mandoline or food processor. Place the sweet potato slices at the bottom of the baking dish, making sure that they overlap to completely cover the bottom. They will shrink slightly during cooking, so allow room for this while overlapping.

Bake for 20 minutes, until the sweet potato is soft and starting to brown. Remove from the oven and set aside to cool. Reduce the oven temperature to 325°F.

Finely chop the ham and sprinkle over the sweet potato crust. Sprinkle the cheese over the crust.

Peel and mince the shallot and sprinkle over the crust.

In a large bowl, beat the eggs with the salt, pepper, garlic powder, dry mustard, and cream until just blended. Pour the egg mixture over the crust.

Bake for 45 minutes, or until the eggs are just set. Let stand 10 minutes to cool and serve. Store leftovers in the refrigerator for up to 4 days and reheat before serving.

bacon & egg bistro salad

TOTAL TIME 30 min. | **ACTIVE TIME** 20 min. | **SERVINGS** 4

Salad for breakfast? If you haven't tried it, you are missing out! This salad is often served in restaurants for lunch or dinner, but if I'm putting bacon and eggs on a salad, I'm eating it for breakfast! Let's break the no-salad-for-breakfast stigma!

6 slices bacon

2 tablespoons red wine vinegar

1 teaspoon Dijon mustard

1 tablespoon honey

½ teaspoon freshly ground black pepper

½ teaspoon garlic powder

1 tablespoon white vinegar

4 large eggs

8 ounces baby greens, such as spinach or mesclun lettuce mix

In a large skillet over medium heat, brown the bacon slices until crispy, about 12 minutes. Leaving the grease in the skillet, remove the bacon and place on a paper-towel-lined plate to drain.

Add the red wine vinegar, mustard, honey, pepper, and garlic powder to the skillet and whisk to combine with the bacon grease. Scrape the mixture out of the skillet into a medium bowl and set aside.

Place 2 inches of water in the skillet and add the white vinegar. Bring to a simmer. Carefully crack each egg into a small bowl, leaving the yolk intact. Gently pour each egg into the skillet and cook without moving for about 4 minutes, or until the white is cooked and the yolk is still slightly runny. Remove the eggs carefully with a slotted spoon and let drain on a towel to remove excess water.

Wash and dry the greens and toss with the vinaigrette. Chop the bacon and mix into the bowl with the greens. Divide the greens among four serving bowls. Top each bowl with an egg and serve immediately.

ham & egg breakfast cups

TOTAL TIME 15 min. | **ACTIVE TIME** 5 min. | **MAKES** 12 breakfast cups

Finding healthful breakfast options for busy mornings can be tough, but these ham and egg breakfast cups are a great solution. Easy enough that older kids can help prepare them and they can be premade for even easier use.

12 thinly sliced pieces of deli ham

12 eggs

2 green onions (green part only)

2 ounces feta cheese (optional)

Preheat the oven to 400°F.

Line the cups of a muffin pan with 1 thinly sliced piece of deli ham (folded in half if needed to fit in the muffin pan). Crack 1 egg into each cup.

Bake for 10 to 12 minutes, depending on how firm you like the yolks to be. If you prefer soft or runny yolks, bake for 8 to 10 minutes.

Thinly slice the green onions. Top the eggs with the green onions and, if using, the feta and serve warm.

smoked salmon &
cream cheese frittata

TOTAL TIME 30 min. | **ACTIVE TIME** 15 min. | **SERVINGS** 6

Bagels with smoked salmon and cream cheese were one of my go-to breakfast ideas when I was younger. I love this frittata because it incorporates the smoked salmon and cream cheese into a more nutritious and protein-packed breakfast that can be prepared ahead of time for a quick breakfast on the fly.

12 large eggs

1 teaspoon salt

½ teaspoon freshly ground black pepper

1 teaspoon garlic powder

½ cup heavy cream

2 tablespoons chopped fresh dill or 1 tablespoon dried

2 tablespoons butter

1 medium onion, diced

8 ounces cream cheese

8 ounces smoked salmon

Preheat the oven to 375°F.

Blend the eggs, salt, pepper, and garlic powder with the heavy cream in a blender or whisk together in a medium bowl until combined. Stir the dill into the egg mixture and set aside.

In a large ovenproof skillet, melt the butter over medium heat. Add the onion and sauté 5 to 7 minutes, until translucent. Evenly spread the onion in the skillet. Cut the cream cheese into small cubes and place evenly over the onion mixture, then dice the salmon and place on top.

Carefully pour the egg mixture over the onion, cream cheese, and salmon mixture in the pan. Use a spatula to evenly distribute the salmon and cream cheese. Cook over medium heat for about 2 minutes, or until the edges and bottom are barely set.

Place the skillet in the oven and bake for 8 to 10 minutes, until the center is just set.

Remove, cool for 5 minutes, and serve.

spinach, feta & onion frittata

TOTAL TIME 25 min. | **ACTIVE TIME** 10 min. | **SERVINGS** 4

This frittata combines several of my favorite salad ingredients in a delicious egg base that is great for breakfast or dinner. Frittatas are a simple and fast way to prepare eggs for our whole family on a busy morning and a delicious way to start the day with protein and vegetables!

¼ **cup olive oil**

1 **small onion, diced**

5 **ounces baby spinach**

8 **large eggs**

½ **teaspoon salt**

½ **teaspoon white or freshly ground black pepper**

½ **teaspoon garlic powder**

½ **cup crumbled feta cheese**

Preheat the oven to 400°F.

In a large ovenproof skillet (I use well-seasoned cast iron), heat the oil over medium heat. Add the onion and sauté until it becomes translucent, about 3 minutes. Wash, dry, and roughly chop the spinach and add to the pan with the onion. Sauté until just wilted, about 2 minutes. Beat the eggs in a medium bowl with 2 tablespoons water, the salt, pepper, and garlic powder.

Sprinkle the feta over the vegetable mixture and then carefully pour the egg mixture on top. Use a spatula to evenly distribute the vegetables throughout the egg mixture and let the eggs cook for about 2 minutes, or until the edges are just starting to set. Transfer the skillet to the oven and bake for 10 to 12 minutes, until the center of the egg mixture is set. Remove and let cool for 5 minutes before slicing into wedges to serve.

west texas omelet

TOTAL TIME 10 min.   **ACTIVE TIME** 10 min.   **SERVINGS** 2

I met my husband on a cross-country walking road trip with some other students and this omelet is a remake of one we had in a small diner in West Texas one morning after walking through the night. We were hungry and exhausted and it was perhaps the best omelet we'd ever had!

4 large eggs

½ teaspoon salt

¼ teaspoon freshly ground black pepper

1 tablespoon coconut oil

¼ cup finely chopped green bell pepper

¼ cup finely chopped onion

¼ cup chopped baked ham or cooked bacon

¼ cup grated Cheddar cheese (optional)

Beat the eggs in a small bowl with the salt and pepper. Add about 1 teaspoon of water and beat again until smooth. Set aside.

In a large flat-bottom skillet or omelet pan, heat the oil over medium heat. Add the bell pepper and onion and sauté over medium heat for 2 to 3 minutes, until the vegetables start to soften. Add the ham and sauté an additional 2 minutes. Reduce the heat to medium-low and make sure that the vegetable and ham mixture is evenly distributed around the skillet.

Pour the eggs over the vegetable and ham mixture and cook for 1 to 2 minutes, until the eggs have set. Carefully fold the omelet in half and transfer to a plate. Top with the cheese, if using, and serve.

simple sausage balls

TOTAL TIME 25 min.   ACTIVE TIME 5 min.   SERVINGS 4

Sausage balls were a party food when I was growing up, but I prefer them as a hearty on-the-go breakfast. I recommend making double or triple batches and freezing them for busy mornings.

1 pound ground sausage, preferably spicy

2 cups almond flour

1 tablespoon coconut flour

1 teaspoon garlic powder

10 ounces sharp cheddar cheese, grated

1 large egg

Preheat the oven to 400°F. Grease with butter or line a baking sheet with parchment paper and set aside.

Place all the ingredients in a medium bowl and mix until combined. Form into 1-inch balls and place on the prepared baking sheet.

Bake for 18 to 20 minutes, until the sausage has completely browned and cooked through. Remove from the oven and serve hot. Store leftovers in the refrigerator for up to 4 days and reheat before serving.

sausage sweet potato hash with brussels sprouts

TOTAL TIME 35 min.   **ACTIVE TIME** 30 min.   **SERVINGS** 4

Sweet potatoes make everything better and this delicious and hearty breakfast recipe packs a beneficial punch of protein, healthful carbohydrates, and vegetables for a well-rounded start to the day that doesn't involve anything from a box!

1 pound ground pork sausage

2 large sweet potatoes

2 teaspoons salt

1 teaspoon freshly ground black pepper

1 teaspoon garlic powder

½ pound Brussels sprouts, trimmed

1 tablespoon unsalted butter or coconut oil (optional)

In a large skillet over medium-high heat, brown the sausage, breaking it up as it cooks, for 8 to 10 minutes, or until browned. Remove the skillet from the heat and use a slotted spoon to transfer the sausage to a paper-towel-lined plate to drain. Leave the grease in the skillet.

Peel the sweet potatoes and chop into ½-inch cubes. Add to the skillet and sprinkle with the salt, pepper, and garlic powder. Add about ¼ cup water and turn the heat to medium. Cover and cook for 10 to 12 minutes, until the potatoes have softened. Remove the cover and let all the water cook off and the potatoes start to brown slightly, about 5 to 7 minutes.

Thinly slice the Brussels sprouts and add to the skillet. You might need to add butter, if needed, at this point to avoid sticking. Cook for another 6 to 8 minutes, until the Brussels sprouts have softened. Serve immediately or store in the refrigerator for up to 3 days. Reheat before serving.

make-ahead kitchen sink breakfast bowls

TOTAL TIME 1 hr.   **ACTIVE TIME** 25 min.   **SERVINGS** 8

It can be tough to find healthful breakfast options that can be heated up quickly and that don't come out of a box or package. I'll often premake big batches of these "breakfast bowls" that are a smorgasbord of breakfast foods, freeze them, and quickly reheat them on busy mornings.

4 pounds sweet potatoes

¼ cup coconut oil, melted

1 teaspoon salt

1 teaspoon freshly ground black pepper

1 teaspoon garlic powder

1 pound ground sausage

1 large onion, diced

1 red bell pepper, cored, seeded, and diced

12 large eggs

2 cups salsa

2 cups grated Cheddar cheese (optional)

Preheat the oven to 400°F.

Wash the sweet potatoes and chop into ½-inch cubes. You can peel if desired, but I leave the skin on. Place the potatoes on a large baking sheet and toss with the oil. Sprinkle evenly with the salt, pepper, and garlic powder. Roast for 40 to 45 minutes, until tender in the middle. Brown the sausage in a medium skillet over medium heat for 8 to 10 minutes, breaking it up as it cooks. Remove the skillet from the heat and transfer the sausage to a paper-towel-lined plate. Leave the grease in the skillet. Return the skillet to medium heat and sauté the onion and pepper for 5 to 7 minutes, or until the onion is translucent. Add the eggs to the skillet and scramble until mostly cooked, about 4 to 5 minutes. Do not overcook, especially if you are making this recipe ahead, as the eggs will finish cooking while reheating. Return the sausage to the skillet and stir to combine.

To serve immediately, spoon the sweet potato mixture into eight bowls and top with the egg mixture, salsa, and cheese. To store, spoon the sweet potatoes and egg mixture evenly into eight ovenproof glass containers with lids. Store in an airtight container in the refrigerator for up to 3 days or freeze for up to 2 months, until ready to use. Remove, let defrost, and reheat in the oven, until warm. Top with the salsa and cheese and serve.

ten-minute blender
banana waffles

TOTAL TIME 20 min. | ACTIVE TIME 10 min. | SERVINGS 4

What could be simpler than making waffles in the blender? These are made with bananas, coconut flour, and almond flour for fluffy and naturally sweet waffles— and you can make them in just minutes!

2 overripe bananas

4 eggs

½ cup coconut flour, plus more if needed

½ cup almond flour

1 cup Coconut Milk (page 278) or whole milk

½ teaspoon baking soda

1 tablespoon vanilla extract

1 teaspoon ground cinnamon

¼ cup pure maple syrup, for serving

Preheat the waffle iron.

Place the bananas, eggs, coconut and almond flours, coconut milk, baking soda, vanilla, and cinnamon in a blender and pulse until smooth. Let the batter sit for 5 minutes to allow the flours to absorb the liquid. Coconut and almond flours can vary by brand, so if the mixture is too thin, add 1 additional tablespoon of coconut flour. If too thick, add extra coconut milk.

The final mixture should be thick and scoopable but not pourable. Lightly grease the waffle iron with coconut oil or butter using a brush. Scoop enough waffle batter into the waffle iron to fill (amount will vary by waffle maker). Bake for 2 to 4 minutes, until golden brown. Repeat until all the batter is used. Serve with maple syrup on the side. Fresh fruit makes a nice accompaniment.

orange julius smoothie

TOTAL TIME 5 min. | **ACTIVE TIME** 5 min. | **SERVINGS** 2

An Orange Julius is a creamy orange juice drink that was rumored to have been created at a Los Angeles orange juice stand in the 1920s by a man named Julius. Almost a century later, and this classic drink is going strong. Seems strange to blend milk and orange juice, but this one is well worth a try!

3 oranges

1 cup ice

1 cup Coconut Milk (page 278) or whole milk

1 tablespoon honey

1 teaspoon vanilla extract

1 tablespoon collagen powder (optional but recommended for protein)

Peel the oranges and remove any seeds. Place in a blender, add the remaining ingredients, and blend until smooth.

berry powerful smoothie

TOTAL TIME 5 min. **ACTIVE TIME** 5 min. **SERVINGS** 2

This delicious smoothie is packed with antioxidants and flavor and sweetened naturally with banana and optional maple syrup or honey. The addition of collagen powder makes this a filling breakfast.

1 orange

2 cups mixed fresh or frozen berries

1 frozen banana

1 cup Homemade Yogurt (page 84) or ½ cup Coconut Milk (page 278)

1 tablespoon pure maple syrup or honey

1 tablespoon collagen powder (optional)

Peel the orange and remove any seeds. Place all the ingredients in a blender and blend at high speed until smooth.

gorilla green smoothie

TOTAL TIME 5 min.	ACTIVE TIME 5 min.	SERVINGS 2

Named by my younger son, this smoothie combines delicious tropical fruits with protein-rich chia seeds and sneaky spinach for a sweet green treat with a protein punch.

1 orange

2 cups baby spinach

2 cups Coconut Milk (page 278) or Almond Milk (page 278)

1 cup frozen pineapple

1 frozen banana

2 tablespoons chia seeds

1 tablespoon collagen powder (optional)

Peel the orange, remove any seeds, and place in the blender. Wash and dry the spinach and add to the blender with the remaining ingredients. Blend until smooth.

angel food cake smoothie

TOTAL TIME 5 min. | **ACTIVE TIME** 5 min. | **SERVINGS** 4

A re-creation of my kids' favorite smoothie at a local smoothie bar, this delicious smoothie combines bananas and strawberries with vanilla to mimic the taste of homemade angel food cake.

2 frozen bananas

2 cups fresh or thawed frozen strawberries

2 cups Coconut Milk (page 278) or whole milk

2 tablespoons honey

½ teaspoon vanilla extract

1 tablespoon collagen powder (optional)

Combine all the ingredients in a blender and blend until smooth. Add more milk if needed to reach the desired consistency.

mocha protein smoothie

TOTAL TIME 5 min.   **ACTIVE TIME** 5 min.   **SERVINGS** 1

This is one of my personal favorite morning smoothies. The coffee and chocolate combination gives a natural boost of energy with protein to help keep hunger at bay!

2 tablespoons Medjool dates or 2 tablespoons honey

1 cup cold-brew coffee

1 cup Coconut Milk (page 278)

2 tablespoons gelatin powder

1 tablespoon cocoa powder

2 tablespoons chia seeds

1 cup ice

Remove the pits from the dates and discard. Place the dates in a blender and add the remaining ingredients. Blend until smooth.

peaches & cream smoothie

TOTAL TIME 5 min. | **ACTIVE TIME** 5 min. | **SERVINGS** 1

We always look forward to peach season, and for the month that fresh peaches are abundant, we eat them daily. This is a favorite breakfast.

2 large ripe peaches

1½ cups Coconut Milk (page 278) or whole milk

½ cup Homemade Yogurt (page 84) or store-bought whole milk yogurt

1 tablespoon honey, or more to taste

Pinch of ground cinnamon

1 teaspoon vanilla extract

1 tablespoon collagen powder or vanilla protein powder (optional)

½ cup ice

Peel the peaches and remove and discard the pits. Place the peaches in a blender, add the remaining ingredients, and blend until smooth.

tip: To make this smoothie dairy-free, replace the yogurt with an equal amount of coconut cream or coconut milk yogurt.

berry-chia breakfast crisp

TOTAL TIME 40 min. | **ACTIVE TIME** 10 min. | **SERVINGS** 6

A delicious warm meat-free breakfast with protein from chia seeds, almond flour, and pecans. This hearty fruit crisp is a favorite with my kids and a great way to start the morning.

6 cups frozen berries, defrosted, with liquid

¼ cup chia seeds plus 2 tablespoons

¼ cup pure maple syrup or honey

2 cups almond flour

¼ cup coconut oil

1 teaspoon vanilla extract

1 cup pecans

Preheat the oven to 350°F. Grease a 9 × 13-inch baking dish with butter or coconut oil. Pour the berries and their liquid into the prepared baking dish and sprinkle the ¼ cup chia seeds evenly over the berries, stirring slightly to mix evenly into the fruit. Evenly pour the maple syrup over the top.

In a food processor or blender, pulse together the flour and oil until crumbly. Add the vanilla, the 2 tablespoons chia seeds, and pecans and pulse until the pecans are just chopped. Crumble the flour-nut mixture over the berry mixture in the baking dish and bake for 30 to 35 minutes, until the top is golden brown and the edges are bubbling. Remove, let cool, and serve. Store leftovers in the refrigerator for up to 3 days and reheat before serving.

tip: I often make this crisp first thing in the morning and place it in the oven before I get in the shower. It is ready to serve when I'm done showering and the kids are awake.

homemade yogurt

| **TOTAL TIME** 24 min. | **ACTIVE TIME** 15 min. | **MAKES** 8 cups |

Did you know that yogurt doesn't have to come out of a disposable plastic container? You can make your own at home, very inexpensively, and avoid the additives often found in store-bought yogurt! To make this recipe, be sure to have at least two 1-quart sterile canning jars with lids before you begin.

½ **gallon whole milk, preferably raw**

4 tablespoons of starter culture or premade plain whole milk yogurt

Honey, maple syrup, or fruit for flavor (optional)

Heat the milk in a stainless-steel pot over medium heat until it reaches 180°F.

Pour the heated milk into canning jars and cool, either by setting on the counter or in a cool-water bath until the temperature drops to 115°F. Add the starter culture. Lightly stir just enough to incorporate into the milk. Place the jars in the oven (temperature off) with the light on for 12 to 24 hours.

The light should provide a consistent heat of about 110°F. Put the jars into the refrigerator for 12 hours, until the yogurt is cold and set. Once the yogurt is set, you can pour off the liquid whey from the top or strain the yogurt through cheesecloth for a thicker consistency. Add honey or maple syrup as a sweetener, if desired, or top with fruit before serving. Store in the refrigerator for up to 2 weeks in an airtight container.

gorgeous grape gell-o

TOTAL TIME 3 hr. 5 min.   **ACTIVE TIME** 5 min.   **SERVINGS** 8+

Jell-O is a kid-favorite, and while the boxed version, laden with food dye and sweeteners, leaves a lot to be desired, this is one of the easiest kid favorites to re-create. Real gelatin is a good source of protein and contains beneficial amino acids, and grape juice is hydrating and refreshing.

1¾ cups grape juice (not from concentrate)

1 tablespoon gelatin powder

¼ cup boiling water

Pour ¼ cup of the grape juice into a medium bowl and sprinkle the gelatin powder over it. Whisk quickly as it will set. This will "bloom" the gelatin and help it incorporate more easily. Immediately whisk in the boiling water until combined. Add the remaining 1½ cups juice and whisk until smooth.

Pour the mixture into molds or a loaf pan lined with parchment paper and place in the refrigerator for at least 3 hours to set.

tip: If you want to make a larger batch, double the recipe and pour into a greased or parchment-paper-lined 8 × 8-inch baking dish. Let cool as usual and slice into small cubes. Store in an airtight container in the refrigerator.

piña colada fruit salad

TOTAL TIME 10 min. | **ACTIVE TIME** 10 min. | **SERVINGS** 4

As moms, we may wish that every day could begin with a piña colada on a warm beach, but since it can't, we can at least incorporate the flavors with this delicious fruit salad.

1 pineapple

½ pound fresh strawberries

½ pound red grapes

1 pint fresh blueberries

¼ cup Coconut Milk (page 278) or whole milk

Zest and juice of 1 organic orange

1 tablespoon honey

2 tablespoons unsweetened coconut flakes (optional)

Core the pineapple and chop into ½-inch pieces and place in a bowl. Reserve ¼ cup of the pineapple chunks for the dressing. Wash and slice the strawberries and grapes in half and add to the bowl with the pineapple. Wash and add the blueberries to the bowl.

In a blender, combine the coconut milk, reserved ¼ cup of pineapple chunks, orange zest and juice, and honey and blend until smooth.

Toss the blended sauce with the fruit mixture to coat and top with the coconut flakes, if using. Chill until ready to serve. Store leftovers in the refrigerator for up to 2 days in an airtight container.

salads & sides

It's difficult to think anything but pleasant
thoughts while eating a homegrown tomato.

—LEWIS GRIZZARD

roasted garlic cabbage

TOTAL TIME 40 min.	**ACTIVE TIME** 5 min.	**SERVINGS** 4 to 6

Cabbage is an inexpensive vegetable that makes a delicious addition to recipes but also stands well on its own. This simple recipe is one of my favorite ways to prepare cabbage because it allows the natural flavor of the cabbage to shine.

1 large head of cabbage

3 tablespoons coconut oil or tallow, melted

1 tablespoon sea salt, or to taste

1 tablespoon freshly ground black pepper, or to taste

1 teaspoon garlic powder

Preheat the oven to 400°F.

Slice the cabbage starting at the top of the head so that the slices go against the grain of the leaves, creating a circular pattern within the slices. Aim for ¼- to ½-inch-thick slices.

Grease a baking sheet with 1 tablespoon of the oil. Place the cabbage on the baking sheet and drizzle with the remaining oil. Sprinkle with the salt, pepper, and garlic powder. Roast for 35 to 40 minutes, until tender in the middle and the sides are just starting to turn golden brown. Remove and serve. I enjoy this plain or topped with an over-easy egg for breakfast.

butter-baked acorn squash

TOTAL TIME 1 hr. 40 min. **ACTIVE TIME** 10 min. **SERVINGS** 4

Acorn squash is a great addition to meals in the fall and winter, when it is plentiful and inexpensive. Baking it with butter, salt, and herbs brings out the natural flavors.

2 acorn squash

8 tablespoons (1 stick) unsalted butter or ½ cup coconut oil

2 teaspoons salt

¼ cup pure maple syrup (optional)

1 tablespoon minced fresh parsley or 2 teaspoons dried

Preheat the oven to 375°F.

Cut the squash in half lengthwise and scoop out the seeds and fibers. Use a sharp knife to cut a cross-hatch pattern into the squash. Cut the butter into tablespoons and evenly rub the pats of butter inside each squash half, making sure to coat the slits you just cut. Sprinkle with salt and, if using, drizzle with maple syrup. Sprinkle with the parsley.

Lay the squash cut side up in a large baking dish. Add 1 inch of water to the dish to prevent burning. Lightly cover the dish with foil or, preferably, a glass ovenproof lid. Bake for 60 to 90 minutes, until the flesh is completely soft. Check every 20 to 30 minutes for doneness and to make sure there is still water in the bottom of the pan. Serve in halves or cut each half into thinner slices. Store leftovers in the refrigerator for up to 4 days and reheat before serving.

creamy cucumber-dill salad

TOTAL TIME 10 min. | **ACTIVE TIME** 10 min. | **SERVINGS** 4

A great recipe in the summer months when cucumbers are in season. I recruit my kids to help slice the cucumbers for this recipe and mix the simple tangy marinade with flavors of sour cream, lemon, and dill.

2 medium cucumbers

½ cup sour cream

Juice of 1 lemon

½ teaspoon salt

½ teaspoon freshly ground black pepper

2 tablespoons chopped fresh dill or 1 tablespoon dried

Peel the cucumbers only if desired, thinly slice, and place them in a large bowl. In a small bowl, whisk together the sour cream, lemon juice, salt, pepper, and dill. Pour the sour cream mixture over the cucumbers and toss gently to combine.

Best served immediately, but can be stored in the refrigerator in an airtight container for up to 24 hours before serving.

grapefruit & avocado
salad

TOTAL TIME 10 min.   **ACTIVE TIME** 10 min.   **SERVINGS** 4

Grapefruit and avocado complement each other perfectly in this simple salad. The healthful fats in the avocados and the natural sweetness and tanginess of the grapefruit meld wonderfully for a filling and delicious salad.

2 ripe avocados

3 large ruby red grapefruit

½ teaspoon salt

Zest and juice of 1 organic lime

1 teaspoon pure maple syrup or honey

Halve the avocados, remove the pits, scoop out the flesh, and cut it into large slices. Supreme the grapefruit and reserve any juice (cut over a bowl to do this).

Arrange the avocado and grapefruit slices in an alternating pattern on a platter. Sprinkle with the salt and then drizzle with the lime juice, maple syrup, and reserved grapefruit juice. Top with the lime zest.

braised leeks & carrots

TOTAL TIME 30 min. | **ACTIVE TIME** 5 min. | **SERVINGS** 6

If leeks aren't a regular addition to your meal plan rotation, they should be. Full of flavor without being overpowering, leeks go really well with the natural sweetness of carrots in this simple side dish.

2 pounds leeks

½ pound carrots

1 cup Chicken Bone Broth (page 152) or store-bought

1 teaspoon salt

1 teaspoon white pepper

1 tablespoon minced fresh tarragon

4 tablespoons (½ stick) unsalted butter

Remove the outer layer of the leeks and trim off the roots and the tough parts of the green ends. Cut the leeks into quarters lengthwise and wash well.

If using small carrots, leave whole. If the carrots are large, quarter them. Place the leeks and carrots in a large pan or skillet. Add the broth, salt, and pepper and bring to a simmer. Cover and simmer on medium until the vegetables have softened, about 20 minutes.

Remove the cover and add the tarragon and butter. Let the butter melt, then simmer for another 5 to 10 minutes, until the broth has evaporated.

french grated carrot salad with raisins

TOTAL TIME 10 min. | **ACTIVE TIME** 10 min. | **SERVINGS** 4

Carrot salad is a classic French dish and this version adds pecans and raisins, often found in other carrot salad recipes, along with a classic French vinaigrette.

1 pound carrots

1 cup raisins

Zest and juice of 1 organic lemon

¼ cup orange juice

1 teaspoon Dijon mustard

1 tablespoon white wine vinegar or apple cider vinegar

2 tablespoons olive oil

½ teaspoon salt

Freshly ground black pepper

2 tablespoons pure maple syrup, or more to taste

½ cup chopped pecans

Use a food processor to grate the carrots. Place them in a medium bowl and add the raisins.

In a small bowl, whisk together the lemon zest and juice, orange juice, mustard, vinegar, oil, salt, pepper, and maple syrup until smooth. Pour the mixture over the carrots and raisins. Sprinkle with the chopped pecans and toss to combine.

For best taste, let sit overnight in the refrigerator for the flavors to meld, and serve cold.

steakhouse chop salad

TOTAL TIME 15 min.   ACTIVE TIME 15 min.   SERVINGS 4

A simple and hearty salad that pairs well with steak. This recipe was inspired by one of my favorite dishes at a local restaurant and I often re-create it at home and serve with steak for a very quick but fancy meal.

2 heads of romaine lettuce

4 ounces fresh spinach

1 small red onion

1 large cucumber

4 medium radishes

4 ounces baked ham

1 cup crumbled blue cheese

½ cup sliced almonds, toasted

¾ cup sour cream

¼ cup Homemade Mayonnaise (page 320)

1 teaspoon Dijon mustard

½ teaspoon garlic powder

1 tablespoon lemon juice

1 teaspoon freshly ground black pepper

1 tablespoon minced fresh dill

3 green onions

Wash and finely chop the lettuce and spinach and place in a large bowl. Very thinly slice the red onion, then thinly slice the cucumber and radishes and add to the bowl. Chop the ham into small pieces and add to the bowl. Sprinkle the blue cheese over the vegetables, add the toasted almonds, and toss to combine.

In a small bowl, whisk together the sour cream, mayo, mustard, garlic powder, lemon juice, pepper, and dill until smooth. Thinly slice the green onions (white and green parts) and add to the mixture. Stir to combine and pour over the lettuce mixture. Toss to combine and serve.

sweet potato casserole

TOTAL TIME 1 hr. | **ACTIVE TIME** 15 min. | **SERVINGS** 12

This is a more nutritious version of the classic sweet potato casserole with added beneficial fat from butter or coconut oil and protein from pecans and almond flour. This dish is a regular for our Thanksgiving menu and I make it every few weeks during the fall and winter months.

4 pounds sweet potatoes, peeled

1 teaspoon salt

1½ sticks unsalted butter or 1 cup coconut oil

¼ cup Coconut Milk (page 278) or full-fat store-bought

½ teaspoon vanilla extract

2 cups pecans

½ cup almond flour

½ cup honey or maple syrup

Preheat the oven to 325°F. Grease a 9 × 13-inch baking dish with butter and set aside.

Fill a large stockpot with several quarts of water and bring to a boil. Place the sweet potatoes in the pot and cook over high heat until tender; drain and mash.

In a large bowl, blend the sweet potatoes, salt, 1 stick of the butter (or ½ cup of the oil), coconut milk, and vanilla with an immersion blender or hand mixer until smooth. Pour evenly into the prepared baking dish and set aside.

Finely chop the pecans. In a medium bowl, mix the pecans, the remaining ½ stick butter (or ½ cup oil), flour, and honey by hand until crumbly. Sprinkle the mixture over the sweet potato mixture. Bake for 30 minutes, or until the topping is lightly brown.

chicken caesar salad

TOTAL TIME 35 min. | **ACTIVE TIME** 15 min. | **SERVINGS** 4

Make your own restaurant-style chicken Caesar salad from scratch in about a half hour with this recipe. The homemade dressing takes this classic and simple salad to a new level!

1 egg yolk, at room temperature (very important it is not cold!)

2 teaspoons white wine vinegar

½ cup olive oil

½ teaspoon dry mustard

1 tablespoon lemon juice

2 garlic cloves, finely crushed

2 teaspoons Worcestershire sauce

1 cup grated Parmesan cheese

Salt and freshly ground black pepper

1 pound skinless, boneless chicken breasts

2 heads of romaine lettuce

In a blender, combine the egg yolk, vinegar, oil, dry mustard, lemon juice, garlic, Worcestershire sauce, 2 tablespoons of the Parmesan cheese, ½ teaspoon salt, and ½ teaspoon pepper and blend on medium speed until creamy. Set aside.

Pound the chicken with a meat hammer until about ½ inch thick. Sprinkle with salt and pepper and brush with 2 tablespoons of the dressing.

Grill on a preheated grill over medium heat for 10 to 15 minutes, until cooked through, or pan-cook in a large skillet with 2 tablespoons of olive oil for about 7 minutes per side, or until the chicken is completely cooked. Set aside the chicken to cool.

Wash, dry, and chop the lettuce and place in a large bowl. When the chicken is cool enough to handle, chop and add to the bowl. Sprinkle the salad mixture with the remaining Parmesan cheese. Pour the dressing over the salad and toss to combine.

tip: To make it dairy-free, omit the Parmesan cheese. This will change the flavor of the finished dish, but the egg-based dressing will provide creaminess.

citrus-infused roasted beet salad

TOTAL TIME 1 hr. 15 min. **ACTIVE TIME** 15 min. **SERVINGS** 4

Beets are a great source of vitamin C, potassium, and folate. While many people ignore these brightly colored root vegetables, they are extremely versatile and with recipes like this one can be a simple addition to any fall menu.

1 bunch of beets (about 6 total)

¼ cup plus 3 tablespoons olive oil

1 teaspoon salt

1 teaspoon freshly ground black pepper

2 organic ruby grapefruit

1 organic lime

1 tablespoon honey

8 ounces fresh spinach

4 ounces goat cheese

½ cup chopped pistachios

Preheat the oven to 400°F.

Cut the greens off the beets, wash them, and set aside to sauté another time. Do not cut off the tops or roots.

Place the beets in an 8 x 8-inch glass baking dish with a glass cover and drizzle with the ¼ cup oil. Sprinkle with the salt and pepper. Add ¼ cup water and cover the baking pan. Roast until the beets are fork tender, about 60 minutes. Remove from the oven and let cool. Cut the beets into wedges and set aside.

Zest the grapefruit into a small bowl. Over the bowl, carefully supreme the grapefruit, allowing the juice to drip in. Set aside the grapefruit segments. Zest and juice the lime into the bowl. Add the 3 tablespoons oil and the honey. Whisk to incorporate and set aside.

Wash and dry the spinach and place on a large serving dish. Arrange the cooled beets and grapefruit segments on top of the spinach. Crumble the goat cheese over the mixture, then sprinkle on the chopped pistachios. Drizzle the entire dish with the citrus vinaigrette. Serve immediately and enjoy.

wilted spinach salad
with chicken & bacon

TOTAL TIME 30 min. ⋮ **ACTIVE TIME** 30 min. ⋮ **SERVINGS** 4

A hearty salad with a perfect mixture of flavors and textures is one of my go-to weeknight meal ideas. Protein from bacon and chicken balance out the delicate wilted spinach while wine vinegar and maple syrup offer a subtle contrast to pull the flavors together.

8 slices bacon

1 pound skinless, boneless chicken thighs

½ teaspoon freshly ground black pepper

1 medium red onion

¼ cup red wine vinegar

1 tablespoon maple syrup

½ teaspoon Dijon mustard

2 pounds spinach

In a large skillet over medium-high heat, brown the bacon until crispy, about 10 minutes. Remove the bacon to a paper-towel-lined plate to drain, but leave the grease in the skillet.

Chop the chicken into bite-size pieces and add to the skillet. Sprinkle with the pepper and cook, stirring often, until cooked through, about 12 minutes.

Meanwhile, finely chop the onion and add to the skillet. Sauté 6 to 8 minutes, until the chicken is completely cooked and the onion is translucent. Add the vinegar to the skillet to deglaze. Stir in the maple syrup and mustard until evenly mixed. Remove from the heat. Chop the bacon and return it to the skillet. Wash and dry the spinach and add to the skillet. Toss to combine and let the spinach wilt slightly. Remove and serve immediately.

tip: If you prefer not to wilt the spinach, instead of adding it to the skillet, plate the spinach and serve the chicken mixture on top.

sesame green beans

TOTAL TIME 15 min. | **ACTIVE TIME** 15 min. | **SERVINGS** 4

Green beans are a simple, nutritious classic vegetable with a long history on dinner tables. This is one of my favorite ways to prepare them, with subtle flavors of sesame and garlic.

1 pound green beans

2 tablespoons sesame seeds

1 teaspoon toasted sesame oil

½ cup Chicken Bone Broth (page 152) or store-bought

½ teaspoon salt

½ teaspoon freshly ground black pepper

1 teaspoon garlic powder

Wash and trim the ends off the green beans. Place the sesame seeds in a large skillet over medium heat and toast, stirring constantly, until they start to brown and become fragrant. Add the oil and green beans to the skillet and sauté for 2 minutes, until the beans are starting to green.

Add the broth to the skillet and sprinkle with the salt, pepper, and garlic powder. Simmer, uncovered, for 8 to 10 minutes, until the green beans are tender and most of the broth has evaporated. Remove from the heat and serve.

wedge salad
with avocado green dressing

TOTAL TIME 25 min. | ACTIVE TIME 25 min. | SERVINGS 4 to 6

A great salad, which I often make for lunch. My kids love the green dressing and this pairs well with leftover chicken or beef for a complete meal in just minutes.

1 head of iceberg lettuce

1 small red onion

2 tomatoes

1 ripe avocado

Zest and juice of 1 organic lemon

¼ cup sour cream or plain whole milk yogurt

1 teaspoon garlic powder

½ teaspoon salt

½ teaspoon freshly ground black pepper

¼ cup minced fresh parsley

2 green onions

8 slices cooked bacon (optional)

Peel the outer leaves off the lettuce and remove the core. Wash, dry, and cut into 4 to 6 wedges and divide among the same number of plates. Thinly slice the onion, chop the tomatoes into bite-size pieces, and divide among the plates.

Halve the avocado, remove the pit, and scoop out the flesh. Place in a blender along with the lemon zest and juice, sour cream, garlic powder, salt, and pepper and blend on high, until creamy.

Mince the parsley and the green onions and fold in with a spatula.

Spoon the green dressing over the lettuce wedges before serving. Chop the bacon, if using, and sprinkle over the top.

roasted sweet potato salad

TOTAL TIME 1 hr. | **ACTIVE TIME** 45 min. | **SERVINGS** 4

I've never been a big fan of regular potato salad, but I absolutely love this sweet potato adaptation, which greatly upgrades the flavor and nutrients.

2 pounds sweet potatoes

1 large onion

¼ cup coconut oil

1 teaspoon salt

½ cup mayonnaise

2 tablespoons white wine vinegar

1 tablespoon honey

½ teaspoon freshly ground black pepper

1 teaspoon garlic powder

Zest and juice of 1 organic orange

4 green onions

Preheat the oven to 400°F.

Peel the sweet potatoes, if desired, and chop into ½ inch chunks. Chop the onion into bite-size pieces.

Place the sweet potatoes and onion on a large baking sheet. Add the oil and toss. Sprinkle with the salt and place in the oven. Roast for 30 to 40 minutes, until tender and golden brown. Remove from the oven and let cool.

In a small bowl, whisk together the mayonnaise, vinegar, honey, pepper, garlic powder, and orange zest and juice.

Thinly slice the green onions. Toss the roasted sweet potatoes with the green onions and vinaigrette. Serve warm or refrigerate and serve cool.

browned butter–glazed radishes

TOTAL TIME 20 min.   ACTIVE TIME 20 min.   SERVINGS 4

I'd never thought to buy or make radishes until my kids asked to grow them in the garden one year when we were picking out seeds, and we ended up with a bumper crop of them! I eventually needed to expand our basic use of slicing them for salads and started experimenting with cooking them. A gentle sauté helps tone down the natural peppery flavor of radishes and makes them a delicious side dish.

1 pound radishes

4 tablespoons (½ stick) unsalted butter

1 teaspoon salt

½ teaspoon freshly ground black pepper

½ teaspoon garlic powder

1 tablespoon white wine vinegar

1 tablespoon honey

¼ cup minced fresh chives

Wash the radishes, remove the tops, and cut into quarters. In a large skillet over medium heat, melt the butter and add the radishes. Sauté for 10 to 15 minutes, until the radishes are soft and the butter has started to brown and get fragrant. Sprinkle with salt, pepper, and garlic powder.

When the radishes are fork tender, add the vinegar to deglaze and then the honey. Stir to combine and simmer until the flavors meld, about 2 minutes. Add the chives to the skillet and stir gently to combine. Remove from the heat and serve immediately.

chopped broccoli salad with grapes

TOTAL TIME 1 hr.　　**ACTIVE TIME** 10 min.　　**SERVINGS** 8

Make basic broccoli salad amazing with red onion, bacon, grapes and raisins, pecans, and Homemade Mayonnaise (page 320). I often make this salad for barbecues and other get-togethers with friends, and it is always a hit!

2 heads of broccoli

1 red onion

½ pound cooked bacon slices

1 pound red grapes

½ cup raisins

½ cup pecans

1 cup Homemade Mayonnaise (page 320) or store-bought

1 tablespoon apple cider vinegar

¼ cup pure maple syrup

½ teaspoon garlic powder

Cut the broccoli florets into bite-size pieces and place in a medium bowl. Finely chop the onion and add to the bowl. Chop the bacon and add to the bowl. Slice the grapes in half and add to the bowl, then sprinkle on the raisins. Toast the pecans if you wish (it's not necessary), roughly chop, and add to the bowl.

In a small bowl, whisk together the mayo, vinegar, maple syrup, and garlic powder. Pour the dressing over the salad and toss to combine. Cover and refrigerate for at least 1 hour before serving to let the flavors meld.

sesame-citrus bok choy salad

TOTAL TIME 15 min. **ACTIVE TIME** 15 min. **SERVINGS** 6

Bok choy is a great source of vitamins C and K and a nutrient-rich but low-calorie member of the cabbage family. It has a milder flavor than cabbage and it shines in this simple salad.

1 pound bok choy

1 large carrot

1 apple

1 red onion

¼ cup raisins

½ cup sunflower seeds, toasted

1 tablespoon sesame seeds

1 tablespoon toasted sesame oil

¼ cup rice wine vinegar

Zest and juice of 1 organic orange

Zest and juice of 1 organic lime

1 tablespoon coconut aminos or wheat-free fermented soy sauce

2 tablespoons pure maple syrup or honey

½ teaspoon salt

½ teaspoon freshly ground black pepper

½ teaspoon garlic powder

Thinly slice the bok choy. You should have at least 4 cups. Peel the carrot, apple, and onion and thinly slice. (I recommend using a peeler to slice the carrot and apple to get thin slivers.) Place all in a large bowl and add the raisins, sunflower seeds, and sesame seeds.

In a small bowl, whisk together the oil, vinegar, orange and lime zests and juices, coconut aminos, maple syrup, salt, pepper, and garlic powder. Pour the dressing over the salad and toss to combine. Serve immediately or let the flavors meld in the refrigerator for 2 hours before serving.

basil–zucchini ribbon salad

TOTAL TIME 20 min. | ACTIVE TIME 20 min. | SERVINGS 8

My spiral vegetable slicer has become one of my favorite kitchen tools because of simple dishes like this. It turns zucchini into flat ribbons that pair perfectly with fresh basil and pine nuts in this easy salad.

2 pounds zucchini

1 bunch of fresh basil

¼ cup olive oil

1 teaspoon Dijon mustard

Zest and juice of 1 organic lime

¼ teaspoon salt

¼ teaspoon freshly ground black pepper

½ teaspoon garlic powder

1 teaspoon honey (optional)

½ cup pine nuts, toasted

Parmesan cheese (optional)

Trim the ends of the zucchini and shave lengthwise into long ribbons using a spiralizer with the ribbon blade (best way), a mandoline on the thinnest setting (easy way), or a vegetable peeler (slower option) and place in a large bowl. Thinly slice the basil leaves and add to the bowl.

In a small bowl, whisk together the oil, mustard, lime zest and juice, salt, pepper, garlic powder, and honey, if using. Pour the dressing over the zucchini and basil and toss to combine. Top with the pine nuts, and, if using, shave the Parmesan cheese over the salad just before serving.

my big fat greek salad

TOTAL TIME 30 min.   **ACTIVE TIME** 15 min.   **SERVINGS** 4

Inspired by one of my favorite movies, this hearty salad combines all of the classic Greek flavors in a single dish. Serve with some leftover chicken for a full meal in minutes.

1 head of romaine lettuce

½ pound tomatoes

1 red onion

1 cucumber

½ pound Kalamata olives, pitted

1 red bell pepper

½ cup crumbled feta cheese

¼ cup olive oil

2 tablespoons red wine vinegar

Zest and juice of 1 organic lemon

½ teaspoon salt

½ teaspoon freshly ground black pepper

1 teaspoon dried oregano leaves

Wash and dry the lettuce, chop, and add to a large bowl. Slice and chop the tomatoes into bite-size pieces and add to the bowl. Very thinly slice the onion and add to the bowl. Cut the cucumber in half lengthwise, then thinly slice and add to the bowl. Drain the olives and add to the bowl. Core, seed, and chop the bell pepper and add to the bowl. Top with the feta cheese and toss to combine.

In a small bowl, whisk together the oil, vinegar, lemon zest and juice, salt, pepper, and oregano. Pour the dressing over the salad and toss to combine. Let sit at room temperature 30 minutes before serving to allow the flavors to meld.

zucchini & summer squash gratin

TOTAL TIME 1 hr. 20 min. | ACTIVE TIME 15 min. | SERVINGS 8

One of my favorite summer recipes when squash, zucchini, and tomatoes are plentiful and inexpensive at the farmers' market. Layers of squash and zucchini are combined with fresh tomatoes and caramelized onions and seasoned with Parmesan cheese and fresh basil. Fragrant and delicious! I always make a double batch and freeze one before baking.

2 large sweet onions

½ cup olive oil, plus more for drizzling

1 pound ripe tomatoes

1 pound yellow squash

1 pound zucchini

1 teaspoon salt

1 teaspoon freshly ground black pepper

1 teaspoon garlic powder

¼ cup minced fresh basil or 2 tablespoons dried

2 cups grated Parmesan cheese

Preheat the oven to 350°F.

Very thinly slice the onions. Heat ¼ cup of the oil in a large skillet and add the onions. Slowly sauté over medium heat until caramelized and fragrant, about 15 minutes. Transfer to a 3-quart gratin dish or 9 × 13-inch baking dish.

Core the tomatoes and thinly slice. Set aside. Very thinly slice the yellow squash and zucchini. Toss with the remaining ¼ cup oil, salt, pepper, and garlic powder. Sprinkle 1 tablespoon of fresh basil or ½ tablespoon of dried basil over the onions in the dish. Place a single layer of the tomato slices over the onions. Sprinkle with ½ cup of the Parmesan cheese and

basil. Repeat with a layer of zucchini and then a layer of yellow squash, sprinkling each layer with cheese and basil. Continue layering until the dish is full. Sprinkle the top with the remaining Parmesan cheese and basil. Drizzle with extra oil if desired.

Bake for 60 minutes until the squash in the middle is tender, the top and edges have browned, and the mixture has reduced.

Let cool and serve. Or cover tightly and freeze for up to two months. Defrost overnight in the refrigerator and reheat before serving.

tuscan turnip gratin

TOTAL TIME 50 min. **ACTIVE TIME** 20 min. **SERVINGS** 8

Turnips can be incredibly delicious and sweet when prepared correctly. This simple gratin adds the Tuscan flavors of fennel, garlic, basil, and oregano for a rustic and delicious side.

2 pounds turnips

1 large fennel bulb

4 garlic cloves

1 cup heavy cream or Coconut Milk (page 278)

1 teaspoon salt

1 teaspoon white or freshly ground black pepper

1 tablespoon dried basil

1 teaspoon dried oregano

4 tablespoons (½ stick) unsalted butter

1 cup grated Parmesan cheese (optional)

Preheat the oven to 400°F.

Peel the turnips. Using a mandoline (preferred) or very sharp knife, slice the turnips as close to paper thin as possible. Place in a medium bowl and set aside. Peel the fennel, trim off the ends, and thinly slice. Set aside in a small bowl. Mince the garlic.

Pour the cream into a large ovenproof skillet and add the garlic, salt, pepper, basil, and oregano. Bring to a boil and turn off the heat. Pour the cream mixture into a small bowl and set aside.

Wipe out the skillet and add the butter to it. Melt the butter over medium heat, then turn off the heat. Place about one-third of the turnip slices in the skillet. Add a layer of about one-third of the fennel slices. Sprinkle with one-third of the Parmesan cheese, if using, and pour one-third of the cream mixture over this. Repeat two more times until all the turnips, fennel, cream mixture, and Parmesan cheese have been used.

Cover the skillet and cook on medium heat on the stovetop for 10 to 12 minutes, until the cream is bubbling. Reduce the heat to medium-low and simmer, covered, for 20 to 25 more minutes, until the turnips are tender.

Remove the cover and bake for 12 minutes, or until the top has browned. Remove from the oven, let cool for 5 minutes, and serve.

oven-roasted rutabaga

TOTAL TIME 55 min. | **ACTIVE TIME** 10 min. | **SERVINGS** 6

Rutabagas are a root vegetable and a member of the cabbage family. They store well and many people use them as a lower-carb replacement for potatoes in dishes. We often use them in soups or hash browns and love this simple oven-roasted version.

2 large rutabagas

¼ cup olive oil, plus more if needed

2 teaspoons salt

1 teaspoon freshly ground black pepper

1 teaspoon garlic powder

1 tablespoon chopped fresh parsley

Zest and juice of 1 organic lemon

Preheat the oven to 400°F.

Peel the rutabagas and chop into ½-inch cubes. Toss with the oil, salt, pepper, and garlic powder and spread in a single layer on a large baking sheet.

Roast for 45 minutes, or until the rutabagas are tender and browned. Remove from the oven, and while still warm, sprinkle the parsley and lemon zest over the roasted rutabagas. Right before serving, sprinkle the lemon juice over the top.

kohlrabi fritters with avocado-dill sauce

TOTAL TIME 20 min. | **ACTIVE TIME** 10 min. | **SERVINGS** 6

Kohlrabi is a type of cabbage with a thick center that holds up well in cooked dishes. I love to add it to soups, but these fritters are a kid favorite at our house, especially when topped with avocado-dill sauce. Give this unusual and delicious vegetable a try!

1 ripe avocado

½ cup Greek yogurt

Zest and juice of 1 organic lemon

¼ cup finely minced dill

1 teaspoon garlic powder

2 large kohlrabi bulbs

1 large onion

4 eggs

1 teaspoon salt

½ teaspoon freshly ground black pepper

1 teaspoon garlic powder

½ teaspoon ground cayenne pepper

½ cup arrowroot powder or flour, plus more if needed

Coconut oil, for frying

Halve the avocado, remove the pit, scoop out the flesh, and place in a food processor. Add the yogurt and blend until smooth. Stir in the lemon zest and juice, dill, and garlic powder and set aside.

Peel the kohlrabi with a sharp knife. Grate the kohlrabi and onion with a box grater.

Wrap the grated kohlrabi and onion in a large clean dish towel, twist both ends, and squeeze tightly to remove any excess moisture and wilt the kohlrabi. Place the mixture in a large bowl. Add the eggs, salt, pepper, garlic powder, and cayenne and mix with a large spoon until combined.

Stir in the arrowroot. If there is still liquid visible in the bowl, add more arrowroot to absorb and stir well to combine.

In a large skillet over medium-high heat, heat enough oil so that when melted, you have ¼ inch oil. Scoop out about ⅓ cup of the kohlrabi mixture and form into patties by hand. Fry for 2 to 3 minutes per side, until golden brown, and repeat until the entire mixture has been used. Season lightly with salt and serve topped with the avocado-yogurt sauce.

delicious dinners

For each new morning with its light,
For rest and shelter of the night.
For health and food, for love and friends,
For everything Thy goodness sends.

—RALPH WALDO EMERSON

stuffed sweet potatoes

TOTAL TIME 1 hr.   **ACTIVE TIME** 10 min.   **SERVINGS** 4

This easy-to-make recipe gets rave reviews whenever I serve it and is one of the most loved recipes on my blog and the most requested by my kids. The best part? It is one of the simplest recipes to make and there are endless ways to mix it up!

4 large sweet potatoes

1 pound ground sausage

2 onions

1 bunch of spinach

Coarse sea salt, to taste

½ teaspoon freshly ground black pepper

1 teaspoon garlic powder

½ teaspoon dried sage

1 teaspoon dried basil

Sharp Cheddar cheese (optional)

Sour cream (optional)

Preheat the oven to 350°F.

Bake the sweet potatoes for 45 to 60 minutes, until soft. (You can do this ahead of time and reheat in the oven before stuffing). Remove from the oven.

While the potatoes are baking (or reheating), in a large skillet over medium-high heat, brown the sausage. While the sausage is browning, dice the onions and add. When the onions have started to soften and the sausage has browned, after 7 to 9 minutes, add the spinach to the skillet. Sauté until the spinach has wilted, 3 to 4 minutes, and add the spices.

In a large baking dish or on a baking sheet, slice the top of each sweet potato lengthwise (not cutting entirely through to the bottom) to make a pocket in the top of the sweet potato. Mash gently with a fork to flatten and add a big scoop of the sausage filling to the middle of the sweet potato, evenly dividing among them. Top with cheese, if using. Return to the oven to melt the cheese and incorporate the flavors, about 10 minutes. Top with sour cream, if using, and serve.

stuffed zucchini
sausage boats

TOTAL TIME 50 min.   ｜   ACTIVE TIME 20 min.   ｜   SERVINGS 4

Who says kids can't love vegetables? Mine love to help make (and eat) these stuffed zucchini boats, and I love this simple meal idea that they eat without complaining!

4 medium zucchini

1 tablespoon coconut oil or unsalted butter

1 medium onion, diced

1 red bell pepper, cored, seeded, and diced

1 pound ground beef

½ teaspoon garlic powder

½ teaspoon onion powder (see Note, page 297)

½ teaspoon sea salt

½ teaspoon freshly ground black pepper

½ teaspoon dried basil

½ teaspoon dried thyme

¼ cup chopped roasted red peppers (optional)

2 large eggs

4 slices Cheddar cheese (optional)

½ cup sour cream

Preheat the oven to 375°F.

Bring a large pot of water to a boil. Place the whole zucchini into it and boil until somewhat tender when pierced with a fork, about 10 minutes.

Heat the coconut oil or butter in a large skillet over medium-high heat and cook the onion and bell pepper. After the veggies have cooked for 5 minutes and start to soften, add the beef to brown, breaking it up as it cooks, for another 5 to 7 minutes, or until browned through. Stir in the spices until evenly mixed. Remove from the heat. Once the zucchini are cooked and are cool enough to handle, cut in half lengthwise and scoop out the seeds and some of the flesh to leave a ¼-inch-thick shell.

Place the zucchini on a large baking sheet and add the scooped-out seeds to the meat and veggies mixture. Add the roasted red peppers, if using, and the eggs to the meat mixture and stir well. Stuff equal portions of the meat into the zucchini boats. Top each with a slice of cheese, if using. Bake for 25 to 30 minutes, until well heated and the cheese starts to bubble. Garnish with a dollop of sour cream and serve hot.

shepherd's pie

TOTAL TIME 50 min.   **ACTIVE TIME** 20 min.   **SERVINGS** 4

Shepherd's pie is traditionally made with lamb; when made with beef, it's called cottage pie. But growing up, we called both versions shepherd's pie, and the name has always stuck. My recipe sneaks in nutrient-rich cauliflower in place of white potatoes.

2 pounds ground beef or lamb

Salt and freshly ground black pepper

2 onions

1 tablespoon coconut oil or unsalted butter

1 1-pound bag frozen mixed veggies

3 heads of cauliflower

4 tablespoons (½ stick) unsalted butter

4 ounces cream cheese

1 teaspoon dried basil

1 teaspoon dried oregano

1 teaspoon garlic powder

¼ teaspoon ground cayenne pepper

1 egg

4 ounces mild Cheddar cheese, grated

Preheat the oven to 350°F.

In a large skillet over medium-high heat, brown the beef, breaking it up as it browns, for 8 to 10 minutes. Season to taste with salt and pepper when cooked and remove to a large bowl.

Dice the onions and sauté with the coconut oil in the same skillet you used for the meat over medium heat for 3 to 4 minutes, until somewhat soft. Add to the bowl with the meat.

Pour the mixed veggies in the same skillet over medium heat until defrosted and toss, then add to the same bowl as the meat and onions. Set aside.

Fill a large pot with water and bring to a boil. Add the cauliflower, cover, and cook 5 to 7 minutes, until soft enough to mash. Remove the pot from the heat, pour off the water, and add the butter and cream cheese. Add the basil, oregano, garlic powder, 1 teaspoon salt, 1 teaspoon pepper, and cayenne and mash. (I use an immersion blender to make it really smooth.)

Add the egg to the meat bowl and mix well by hand. Scrape the mixture into a 9 × 13-inch baking dish. Spread the mashed cauliflower mixture over the top until smooth. Bake 30 minutes. Remove from the oven, top with the Cheddar cheese, and bake for 5 more minutes, or until the cheese is bubbly. Remove from the oven, let cool for 5 minutes, and serve warm.

meat loaf cupcakes

TOTAL TIME 45 min.   **ACTIVE TIME** 15 min.   **SERVINGS** 4

Cupcakes have exploded in popularity in recent years with entire bakeries, TV shows, and cookbooks devoted to them. I don't like refined sugar and food dye–infused cupcakes, but the delivery method is brilliant and our family likes this savory and nutrient-rich alternative. In place of sugar and flour, I make a meat loaf with hidden veggies as the base and a whipped sweet potato "frosting" to top.

6 medium sweet potatoes

1 medium onion

2 pounds ground beef

3 eggs

¼ cup almond flour

1 teaspoon dried basil

1 teaspoon garlic powder

2 tablespoons Worcestershire sauce

Sea salt

Freshly ground black pepper

¼ cup coconut oil or 4 tablespoons (½ stick) unsalted butter

Preheat the oven to 375°F.

Pierce the sweet potatoes with a fork and place them in the oven to bake. Alternately, you may peel, cube, and boil them until soft.

Finely dice the onion and place in a large bowl. Add the beef, eggs, flour, basil, garlic powder, Worcestershire sauce, 1 teaspoon salt, and ½ teaspoon pepper. Mix by hand until well incorporated.

Grease the cups of a muffin pan with the oil and divide the mixture among the cups. (You can also just press the mixture in a 9 × 13-inch baking dish.) Place the muffin pan on the middle rack in the oven and put a baking sheet with a rim under it. Bake for 30 to 35 minutes, until the meat is cooked through (add an extra 10 minutes for a 9 x 13 dish).

If you baked the potatoes, slice and remove them from the skin. If you boiled them, remove from the water and strain. Place the potatoes in a large bowl and add the oil and salt and pepper to taste. Mash by hand or use an immersion blender until creamy and smooth.

Remove the meat muffins from the oven when they are cooked through (there should not be any pink in the center) and remove from their cups. Top each with a dollop of the mashed sweet potatoes.

up pasty

TOTAL TIME 1 hr.   ACTIVE TIME 10 min.   SERVINGS 4

Years ago, we visited friends in the Upper Peninsula of Michigan. I offered to help make dinner one night and ended up in a great conversation with their amazing mom. We made something called a pasty. I'd never heard of them, but thanks to the good friends that was one of the most delicious and satisfying meals I've ever eaten. This re-creation brings back memories of our quiet time in the Michigan snow.

2 cups almond flour

½ cup arrowroot powder

¼ cup coconut oil or lard

1 egg

1 tablespoon ice water

1 pound ground beef, bison, or venison

2 large sweet potatoes

1 medium rutabaga

1 onion

2 carrots

1 teaspoon salt

1 teaspoon freshly ground black pepper

1 teaspoon garlic powder

1 teaspoon dried basil

Mix the flour and arrowroot in a food processor. Add the oil and pulse until combined. Add the egg and pulse until smooth. Slowly add the ice water until the dough forms a stiff ball. Remove the dough to a medium bowl and place in the refrigerator.

In a large skillet over medium-high heat, brown the beef, breaking it up as it cooks, for 8 to 10 minutes. Peel and chop the potatoes, rutabaga, onion, and carrots into ¼-inch cubes. Add to the skillet and sauté for about 5 minutes. Add approximately ½ cup water and the spices and simmer until the potatoes and carrots are tender (add more water and continue to simmer if needed). When cooked, remove from the heat and set aside.

Preheat the oven to 375°F. Grease or line a baking sheet with parchment paper and set aside.

Remove the dough from the refrigerator and divide into four pieces. Roll each into an 8- or 9-inch circle. Fill one side of the dough with the filling mixture and fold the other half over to attach. Use a fork to seal the edges and carefully transfer to the prepared baking sheet. Bake for 30 minutes, or until the dough has started to turn golden and the inside is hot. Serve immediately with ketchup (page 315), if desired.

stuffed pumpkin

TOTAL TIME 1 hr.   **ACTIVE TIME** 10 min.   **SERVINGS** 4

Pumpkins have so much more potential than just pie or jack-o'-lanterns and this beta-carotene-rich vegetable can be used in many creative ways! Stuff a pumpkin with ground meat and fall vegetables, like fennel, apple, and onion, for a one-pan meal with a beautiful presentation!

1 pound ground beef

1 medium onion

1 large fennel bulb

1 large leek

2 tablespoons (¼ stick) unsalted butter or coconut oil

1 medium apple

1 teaspoon salt

½ teaspoon freshly ground black pepper

1 teaspoon garlic powder

1 teaspoon dried basil

3 large eggs (optional)

1 medium pumpkin (about 5 pounds) or 2 small (2 to 3 pounds each)

Preheat the oven to 350°F. Grease a large baking dish and set aside.

In a large skillet over medium-high heat, brown the beef, breaking it up as it cooks, for 8 to 10 minutes. Remove the beef from the skillet and set aside.

Finely chop the onion. Peel the fennel, trim off the ends, and thinly slice. Remove the outer layer of the leek, cut off the root and the thick part of the green stem, wash well, and finely chop. Melt the butter over medium heat in the same skillet that was used for the beef. Add the onion, fennel, and leek to the skillet and sauté until all are tender, about 8 minutes. Peel, core, and chop the apple and add to the skillet. Return the beef to the skillet and season with the salt, pepper, garlic powder, and basil. Remove from the heat and let cool slightly. Stir in the eggs, if using.

Carefully cut off the top of the pumpkin and scoop out the seeds and fibers.

Spoon the filling mixture into the pumpkin and place it in the prepared baking dish and bake for approximately 1 hour, until the flesh of the pumpkin is soft. Also, you can save the seeds to roast for a snack or dry them to plant in the garden.

thai beef & napa cabbage salad

TOTAL TIME 30 min.   ACTIVE TIME 12 min.   SERVINGS 4

Years ago, we received eight Napa cabbages in our weekly CSA (Community Supported Agriculture) box and I'd never had to prepare one before. We ate this delicate cabbage in some form every day that week so that none of it would go to waste and this was my favorite of all the variations we tried. The citrus, coconut aminos, cilantro, and ginger provide a complex flavor in this 30-minute recipe!

1 pound beef tenderloin steaks

1 tablespoon olive oil

Zest and juice of 2 limes

Zest and juice of 1 orange

¼ cup coconut aminos or wheat-free fermented soy sauce

1 tablespoon pure maple syrup

1 teaspoon chili sauce

½ cup finely chopped fresh cilantro

1 1-inch piece fresh ginger

4 garlic cloves

1 small head of Napa cabbage

1 cucumber

1 bunch of green onions

1 cup sliced almonds, toasted

Cut the steaks into four pieces. Grill or skillet-cook in the olive oil over medium heat for 5 to 6 minutes per side. Remove from the heat and let cool.

Place the lime and orange zests and juices in a medium bowl. Add the coconut aminos, maple syrup, chili sauce, and cilantro. Peel and mince the ginger and add to the bowl. Mince the garlic, add to the bowl, and whisk to combine.

When the meat has cooled, thinly slice against the grain to at most a ¼-inch thickness and add to the bowl. Toss well in the marinade to coat and place in the refrigerator, covered, for at least 4 hours.

When ready to serve, thinly slice the Napa cabbage and place in a large bowl. Peel and thinly slice the cucumber and add to the bowl. Thinly slice the green onions and add to the bowl.

Pour the meat and marinade mixture over the greens and toss to combine. Top with the toasted almonds and serve.

swedish meatballs

TOTAL TIME 35 min.　　ACTIVE TIME 15 min.　　SERVINGS 4

Swedish meatballs, or Köttbulle, are a small type of meatball that is served with a creamy and flavorful gravy instead of a tomato-based pasta sauce like many other types of meatballs. This recipe was thought to be brought to the United States by Scandinavian immigrants and became a party favorite here in the 1950s.

1 pound ground beef

1 pound ground pork

2 yellow onions

2 large eggs

½ cup almond flour

½ teaspoon salt

½ teaspoon freshly ground black pepper

¼ teaspoon ground nutmeg

½ teaspoon ground allspice

2 teaspoons garlic powder

2 tablespoons unsalted butter (¼ stick) or coconut oil, plus more if needed

2 tablespoons arrowroot

3 cups Beef Bone Broth (page 154) or store-bought

½ cup Coconut Milk (page 278) or heavy cream

Preheat the oven to 400°F.

Place the beef and pork in a medium bowl.

Very finely mince one of the onions and add to the bowl. Add the eggs and flour. Sprinkle the mixture with the salt, pepper, nutmeg, allspice, and 1 teaspoon of the garlic powder and mix by hand until combined. Form into 1-inch meatballs. Place the meatballs on a large baking sheet and bake for 18 to 20 minutes, until the meatballs are golden brown and cooked through.

While the meatballs are baking, finely chop the other onion. In a large skillet over medium-high heat, melt the butter and add the onion. Sauté until translucent and soft, about 5 minutes. Add the remaining 1 teaspoon garlic powder and sprinkle with 1 tablespoon arrowroot. Stir to combine. Stir in the broth and coconut milk. Simmer for 4 to 5 minutes, until the mixture starts to thicken. Add up to 1 more tablespoon arrowroot if needed to thicken. Remove the meatballs from the oven and toss in the gravy and serve.

curried cabbage rolls

TOTAL TIME 1 hr. 45 min.   ACTIVE TIME 30 min.   SERVINGS 4

Cabbage rolls are an inexpensive meal idea with endless variations. Our favorite is this curried version filled with mushrooms and beef.

1 large head of cabbage

1 pound ground beef

2 eggs

1 onion

1 teaspoon garlic powder

1 teaspoon onion powder (see Note, page 297)

1 teaspoon dried basil

1 teaspoon dried thyme

1 teaspoon curry powder

1 teaspoon Himalayan salt or other salt of choice

1 teaspoon fresh ground black pepper

3 cups Beef Bone Broth (page 154) or store-bought

1 8 ounce package white button mushrooms

4 tablespoons coconut oil or unsalted butter

Boil 3 quarts of water in a large stockpot. Carefully peel the leaves off of the cabbage head and place in boiling water for 2 to 3 minutes, or until tender. Place any cabbage that can't be pulled into leaves in a greased 9 x 13-inch ovenproof baking dish or Dutch oven.

Preheat the oven to 375°F.

In a medium bowl, mix together the beef, eggs, onion, garlic powder, onion powder, basil, thyme, curry powder, salt, and pepper. Place a small handful of the beef mixture in the middle of each cabbage leaf and roll up like a burrito. Place the rolled-up stuffed cabbage leaves on top of the cabbage pieces in the baking dish. Pour 2 cups of the broth over the rolls and place in the oven, uncovered, for 45 to 60 minutes, until the meat is cooked through.

Meanwhile, slice the mushrooms. In a medium saucepan over medium heat, heat the oil and sauté the mushrooms for 3 to 5 minutes, until browned. Add the remaining 1 cup broth and bring to a boil. Boil approximately 10 minutes, until the stock starts to reduce. Taste and adjust the seasoning as desired.

Remove the cabbage rolls from the oven and serve on a platter with the mushroom sauce on top.

chicken piccata

TOTAL TIME 35 min.　　**ACTIVE TIME** 35 min.　　**SERVINGS** 4

Lightly breaded chicken is skillet-fried and seasoned with white wine, citrus, and parsley for a fast but sophisticated meal. Piccata is a method of preparing food that originated in Italy but often features veal there. We prefer this chicken version and it is a regular part of our meal rotation.

3 skinless, boneless chicken breasts (about 2 pounds)

¾ cup almond flour

½ teaspoon Himalayan or other sea salt

½ teaspoon freshly ground black pepper

½ teaspoon ground turmeric, or more to taste (optional)

½ teaspoon garlic powder, or more to taste

2 large eggs

8 tablespoons unsalted butter

½ cup dry white wine (optional)

1 lemon

4 tablespoons capers (optional)

¼ cup chopped fresh parsley

1 ounce grated Parmesan cheese

Preheat the oven to 300°F.

Butterfly the chicken: Cut the breasts in half lengthwise and flatten by pounding with a meat hammer or the bottom of a cast-iron skillet until about ¼ to ½ inch thick.

Mix the flour, salt, pepper, turmeric, and garlic powder on a plate.

In a small bowl, beat the eggs with the water until frothy.

Dip the chicken in the egg mixture and let drip well, then into the flour mixture and back into the egg mixture.

In a large skillet over medium-high heat, melt 2 tablespoons of the butter. Cook the chicken for 3 to 4 minutes per side, until browned and no longer pink on the inside. (It may take two rounds to cook all the chicken. Use another 2 tablespoons of the butter for the second round.) Place the chicken on a baking sheet and put in the oven to keep warm. Add the wine, if using, to the skillet to deglaze; otherwise, use water. Halve the lemon and squeeze the juice into the skillet. Thinly slice the other half. Drain and rinse the capers, if using, and add to the skillet. Reduce the mixture by about half and then add in the remaining 4 tablespoons butter, stirring until melted. Remove the chicken from the oven and place on a serving platter. Drizzle some of the sauce over each piece and top with the parsley, and the Parmesan cheese. Garnish with the lemon slices and serve.

schweineschnitzel

TOTAL TIME 30 min.   ACTIVE TIME 10 min.   SERVINGS 4

My husband and I visited Germany shortly after we started dating and got to try many traditional German dishes, including all types of Schnitzels. Schnitzel is any meat that has been tenderized, breaded, and fried and we often make this healthier version by breading in almond and coconut flour and pan-frying.

1 pound pork loin or pork chops

2 large eggs

¼ cup Coconut Milk (page 278) or store-bought

¼ cup almond flour

2 tablespoons coconut flour

1 teaspoon garlic powder

2 teaspoons salt, plus more to taste

½ teaspoon freshly ground black pepper

½ cup coconut oil or tallow

1 lemon

Cut the pork loin into thin (less than ½ inch) pieces and use a meat hammer to pound to about ¼-inch thickness.

In a small bowl, whisk together the eggs and coconut milk. (For an egg-free version, use coconut milk alone or substitute ¼ cup yogurt for the eggs.)

Mix the almond and coconut flours, garlic powder, salt, and pepper in a large bowl or on a plate. Dredge the pork cutlets in the egg mixture, then in the flour mixture. Set aside.

In a large skillet over medium-high heat, heat half of the oil. Working in batches if necessary, add the pork cutlets to the skillet and cook for about 4 minutes per side, or until cooked through (golden brown on the outside and an internal temperature of 160°F). Remove and set on a plate to cool. Sprinkle with extra salt if desired. Halve the lemon and squeeze the juice over the cutlets. Slice the other half into wedges. Serve immediately with fresh greens and lemon wedges.

chicken plantain tamales

TOTAL TIME 1 hr. 30 min. | **ACTIVE TIME** 30 min. | **SERVINGS** 4

Tamales were a comfort food of my youth. Growing up in Texas, tamales were often served at church events or gatherings, and I quickly realized after we moved away that good tamales are hard to find. As the saying goes, "If you want something done right, you have to do it yourself," and I love making tamales from scratch using plantains in place of corn for better flavor!

1 pound skinless, boneless chicken thighs

¼ cup chili powder (see Note, page 297)

4 tablespoons coconut oil (see Note, page 23), butter, or lard

6 medium green plantains or 4 large

18 corn husks or parchment paper

2 teaspoons garlic powder

2 eggs

1 tablespoon coconut flour

1 teaspoon ground cumin

Preheat the oven to 375°F.

Place the chicken in a large baking dish and sprinkle with 1 tablespoon of the chili powder. Drizzle with 2 tablespoons of the oil. Bake for approximately 45 minutes, until cooked through and no longer pink in the middle. Remove to a plate and let cool.

While the chicken is cooking, halfway fill a large stockpot with water and bring to a boil. Slice the plantains into 2-inch pieces and add to the pot. Boil for 15 to 18 minutes, until soft (the middle should be fork tender and the skin easy to remove). Use tongs to remove from the water and let cool.

Leave the hot water in the pot and add the husks to begin to soften. When the plantains are cool enough to handle, peel, and place them in a food processor, then pulse until smooth (or you may blend in a medium bowl with an immersion blender). Add 2 tablespoons of the chili powder and 1 teaspoon of the garlic powder and pulse until mixed. Add the eggs, flour, and remaining oil and pulse until a dough begins to form. If needed, add a little bit of water; you want to form a very stiff but not crumbly dough.

Shred the chicken and place in a medium bowl. Add the remaining 1 tablespoon chili powder, the remaining 1 teaspoon garlic powder, and the cumin and mix well.

When the husks have softened, carefully remove from the water one at a time. Place 1 husk on a cutting board and spread ½ cup of the plantain mixture on it. Top with some of the chicken mixture and spread down the middle.

Carefully roll the husk and fold over one end. Lay flat on a baking sheet. Repeat for the remaining husks. Bake for 15 to 20 minutes on each side. (You can also steam for the same amount of time.)

greek grilled chicken
with tzatziki sauce

TOTAL TIME 1 hr.	ACTIVE TIME 15 min.	SERVINGS 4

Tzatziki sauce . . . oh, tzatziki sauce. Some people think that ketchup makes everything better, but I'd argue that tzatziki trumps ketchup every time. Serve this Greek marinated chicken with tzatziki sauce and a My Big Fat Greek Salad (page 116) for a Mediterranean-inspired meal!

2 pounds skinless, boneless chicken breasts

2 lemons

2 tablespoons olive oil

1½ teaspoons salt

1½ teaspoons garlic powder

1 teaspoon dried marjoram

2 cups Greek yogurt

2 cucumbers, peeled and finely chopped

Zest and juice of 1 organic lemon

1 tablespoon finely minced fresh dill

2 heads romaine lettuce, or 12 leaves, for serving (optional)

1 small red onion, sliced, for serving

1 medium tomato, sliced, for serving

Place the chicken in a glass baking dish and drizzle with the juice of 2 lemons and the oil. Season with 1 teaspoon of the salt, 1 teaspoon of the garlic powder, and the marjoram. Cover and place in the refrigerator. Ideally, let marinate overnight, or at least 2 hours.

In a medium bowl, mix the yogurt, cucumbers, the remaining ½ teaspoon salt, the remaining ½ teaspoon garlic powder, the lemon zest and juice, and dill and place in the refrigerator for at least 2 hours to let the flavors meld.

Preheat a grill on medium or the oven to 375°F.

Grill or bake the chicken until done (about 20 minutes on the grill, or about 45 in the oven, flipping once).

Serve the chicken alone or slice and wrap in washed lettuce leaves, topped with the sauce and the onion and tomato slices.

chicken vesuvio

TOTAL TIME 40 min.   **ACTIVE TIME** 20 min.   **SERVINGS** 4

Despite its Italian name (meaning "village chicken)," this recipe actually originated in Chicago, possibly from a restaurant by the same name. Though it is simple to make, this recipe has complex flavors and smells delicious as it cooks!

1 4-pound chicken

2 teaspoons salt

1 teaspoon freshly ground black pepper

1 teaspoon garlic powder

¼ cup olive oil

1½ pounds parsnips

3 garlic cloves

1 teaspoon dried oregano

1 teaspoon dried thyme

½ cup dry white wine

1 cup Chicken Bone Broth (page 152) or store-bought

8 ounces frozen artichoke hearts

Preheat the oven to 425°F.

Cut the chicken into pieces (legs, breasts, and thighs). Sprinkle with the salt, pepper, and garlic powder.

In a large ovenproof skillet over medium-high heat, warm the oil and add the chicken parts, turning every 5 to 8 minutes, until the outside has browned (in batches if needed). Transfer the chicken to a plate.

Peel and slice the parsnips and add to the same skillet that was used for the chicken with the olive oil. Sauté for about 12 minutes, until they start to soften. Mince the garlic and add to the skillet along with the oregano and thyme.

Add the wine to the skillet to deglaze and then the broth. Add the artichoke hearts and stir until warmed through, about 5 minutes. Return the chicken to the skillet and bring to a boil. Cover and place in the oven. Roast for 20 minutes, until the chicken is completely cooked and the parsnips are softened. Remove from the oven and serve.

dairy-free upside-down pizza

TOTAL TIME 35 min. | **ACTIVE TIME** 10 min. | **SERVINGS** 8

Pizza is an undeniable kid favorite. We like to turn things upside down, literally, with this pizza: Meat makes the crust of this unusual pizza and it is topped with sauce and vegetables. Not dairy-free? Add some mozzarella and Parmesan on top!

1 tablespoon olive oil

1 small onion

4 ounces button mushrooms, thinly sliced

½ cup black olives

1 green bell pepper, cored, seeded, and thinly sliced

2 pounds ground beef

2 eggs

1 teaspoon salt

1 teaspoon freshly ground black pepper

1 tablespoon Italian Seasoning (page 298) or store-bought

1 cup prepared pizza sauce

4 ounces cooked ground Italian sausage, sliced ham, or pepperoni

Preheat the oven to 450°F. Grease a lipped cookie sheet with olive oil and set aside.

Thinly slice the onion, mushrooms, and olives. Place in a medium bowl with the bell pepper and set aside.

Place the beef, eggs, salt, pepper, and Italian seasoning in another medium bowl and mix well by hand until incorporated. Spread the beef mixture onto the prepared cookie sheet. Roll or press the meat onto the cookie sheet. Place in the oven and cook for 10 minutes, or until browned and most of the moisture has cooked off. It will reduce in size quite a bit! Just make sure it is browned around the edges and not pink in the middle.

Remove from the oven and pour off any grease from the meat. Turn on the broiler.

Spread the pasta/pizza sauce over the meat "crust," then top with the sausage/ham/pepperoni and the onion, bell pepper, mushrooms, and olives.

Return the cookie sheet to the oven and watch closely. It will only need to be under the broiler for 6 to 8 minutes. Cook until the toppings are slightly browned. Remove from the oven, let cool for 3 minutes, slice, and serve. This is also really good cold for lunch the next day (or breakfast!). It has a similar texture to real pizza and tastes better, in my opinion.

one-pot meals & soups

One cannot think well, love well, sleep well,
if one has not dined well.

—VIRGINIA WOOLF

beef & cabbage stir-fry

TOTAL TIME 30 min. | **ACTIVE TIME** 10 min. | **SERVINGS** 4

This super simple and protein-packed stir-fry is a go-to in our house. It comes together quickly and is easy to customize, and my older kids love making it on their own.

1 pound ground beef, turkey, or venison

1 teaspoon sea salt

1 teaspoon freshly ground black pepper

1 teaspoon garlic powder

1 teaspoon dried basil

1 teaspoon dried oregano

1 teaspoon dried thyme

2 onions

2 carrots

1 large head of cabbage

In a large skillet or wok, brown the beef, breaking it up as it cooks. Add the salt, pepper, garlic powder, basil, oregano, and thyme as you go.

Thinly slice the onions, grate the carrots, and chop the cabbage.

When the beef is almost completely browned, add the onions and carrots. When the onions and carrots are starting to soften, add the cabbage. Cook about 10 more minutes, stirring often, until the cabbage starts to soften. Taste and adjust the seasoning as desired.

bone broth tutorial
with five variations

Bone broth was once a staple in any kitchen, used in sauces, gravies, and other dishes. It seemed to lose favor when TV dinners and premade packaged foods gained popularity, but it has been making a comeback in recent years as news has spread about the health benefits of this age-old food.

chicken bone broth

SERVINGS 16 (1 gallon)

TOTAL TIME 9 hr.

2 or more pounds chicken bones (from 2 to 3 carcasses) from a quality pastured source

2 chicken feet, for extra gelatin (optional)

1 onion

2 carrots

2 stalks celery

1 tablespoon sea salt, or more to taste (optional)

1 teaspoon peppercorns (optional)

1 teaspoon dried basil (optional)

2 tablespoons apple cider vinegar

1 bunch fresh parsley

2 garlic cloves (optional)

Bring 2 gallons water to a boil in a large stockpot and add the chicken bones and, if using, the chicken feet. Roughly chop the onion, carrots, and celery and add to the pot. Add the salt, peppercorns, basil, and apple cider vinegar. Reduce the heat to a simmer.

During the first hour of simmering, check every 20 minutes and remove the foam and impurities that float to the surface. Use a big spoon to skim off and discard the foamy layer that forms. (Pasture-raised chickens will produce much less of this than conventionally raised animals.)

Simmer for about 8 hours, until the bones have started to soften and the liquid has reduced by about half. During the last 30 minutes, add the parsley and garlic, if using.

Remove from the heat and let cool slightly. Ladle the broth through a fine-mesh strainer to remove all the bits of bone and vegetable. When thoroughly cool, store in a gallon-size airtight glass jar in the refrigerator for up to 5 days, or freeze for up to 2 months.

CURRIED CHICKEN BROTH

BEEF BROTH
FRENCH ONION SOUP

BEEF BONE BROTH

CHICKEN BONE BROTH

beef bone broth

SERVINGS 16 (1 gallon)
TOTAL TIME 13 hr.

2 pounds grass-fed beef bones

1 onion

2 carrots

2 stalks celery

2 tablespoons apple cider vinegar

1 tablespoon or more sea salt

1 teaspoon peppercorns

1 tablespoon fresh or dried basil leaf

Preheat the oven to 375°F.

Line a baking sheet with parchment paper. Arrange the bones on the baking sheet and roast in the oven until browned and fragrant, about 20 minutes.

While the bones are roasting, bring 2 gallons water to a boil in a large stockpot. Roughly chop the onion, carrots, and celery and add to the pot. Add the apple cider vinegar, salt, peppercorns, and basil. Reduce the heat to a simmer.

During the first hour of simmering, check every 20 minutes and remove the impurities that float to the surface. Use a big spoon to skim off and discard the foamy layer that forms. (Grass-fed, healthy animals will produce much less of this than conventionally raised animals.)

Simmer for about 12 hours, until the liquid has reduced by about half and the bones have started to soften. Remove from the heat and let cool slightly. Ladle the broth through a fine-mesh strainer to remove all the bits of bone and vegetable. When thoroughly cool, store in a gallon-size airtight glass jar in the refrigerator for up to 5 days, or freeze for up to 2 months.

fish broth

SERVINGS 8
TOTAL TIME 1.5 hr.

2 carrots

1 onion

2 stalks celery

1 pound fish bones

1 teaspoon salt

½ teaspoon black peppercorns

½ teaspoon garlic powder

Preheat the oven to 375°F. Line a baking sheet with parchment paper. Roughly chop the carrots, onion, and celery and place the vegetables and fish bones on the baking sheet. Roast for up to 10 minutes, until just starting to brown.

Meanwhile, fill a large stockpot with 3 quarts water and bring to a boil. Add the roasted fish bones and vegetables, salt, peppercorns, and garlic powder to the pot. Reduce the heat to a simmer.

Simmer for 60 minutes. Remove from the heat and let cool slightly. Ladle the broth through a fine-mesh strainer. When thoroughly cool, store in a gallon-size airtight glass jar in the refrigerator for up to 4 days, or freeze for up to 9 months.

curried chicken broth

SERVINGS 4
TOTAL TIME 15 min.

1 quart Chicken Bone Broth
(page 152)

1 tablespoon curry powder

1 carrot, grated or very thinly
sliced

3 green onions, very thinly
sliced

Pour the broth into a medium saucepan. Add the curry powder, carrot, and green onions to the pan and bring to a simmer. Simmer for 8 minutes, or until the carrots have softened. Serve immediately or store in an airtight glass container or jar in the refrigerator for up to 4 days.

beef broth
french onion soup

SERVINGS 6
TOTAL TIME 25 min.

2 quarts Beef Bone Broth
(page 154) or store-bought

1 teaspoon Herbes de
Provence (page 303) or store-
bought

1 teaspoon salt

½ teaspoon white or freshly
ground black pepper

3 tablespoons unsalted butter

1 large red onion

1 large yellow onion

3 shallots or 1 more large
yellow onion

½ cup dry white wine

Pour the broth into a large saucepan and bring to a simmer. Add the herbes de Provence, salt, and pepper to the broth.

While the broth is simmering, melt the butter in a large skillet over medium heat. Thinly slice the onions and shallots and add to the skillet. Sauté for 10 to 12 minutes, or until soft, translucent, and fragrant. Add the wine to deglaze and remove from the heat. When the broth has reduced by one-third, about 15 minutes, add the onions and shallots to the saucepan and simmer an additional 5 to 6 minutes, to let the flavors meld. Top with sharp Cheddar or Gruyère cheese or crusty homemade bread, if desired, and serve.

cashew chicken
lettuce wraps

TOTAL TIME 25 min.	ACTIVE TIME 10 min.	SERVINGS 4

This recipe was born of desperation one night when I had nothing defrosted, the pantry was virtually empty, and I was struggling to find something to cook. I chopped up the chicken I had in the fridge and seasoned it to taste. On a whim, I threw in some of the cashews my kids had been snacking on and a little maple syrup and was surprised at how delicious the result was!

¼ cup coconut oil or 4 tablespoons (½ stick) unsalted butter

1 pound skinless, boneless chicken breasts or thighs

1 teaspoon garlic powder

1 teaspoon sea salt

1 teaspoon freshly ground black pepper

1 teaspoon dried basil (optional)

3 tablespoons coconut aminos or wheat-free fermented soy sauce

3 tablespoons pure maple syrup, or more to taste

½ cup cashew pieces, toasted

1 head of butter lettuce

½ small red onion

Heat the oil in a large skillet over medium-high heat. Cut the chicken into bite-size pieces and add to the skillet. Season with the garlic powder, salt, pepper, and, if using, the basil and sauté until the chicken is almost completely cooked and is no longer translucent. Add the coconut aminos and stir until the liquid from the coconut aminos starts to evaporate. Add the maple syrup and continue to stir for another 2 to 3 minutes, until the maple syrup and coconut aminos have cooked down and there is very little liquid left in the pan. Add the cashews and stir until heated. Remove from the heat and allow to cool slightly.

Wash, dry, and separate the lettuce leaves. Thinly slice the onion. Fill each leaf with ⅛ of the chicken mixture and top with the onion before serving.

tip: Substitute 2 minced garlic cloves for the garlic powder if you have it.

one-pan pakistani kima

TOTAL TIME 30 min. | **ACTIVE TIME** 10 min. | **SERVINGS** 4

This recipe has been a regular in my meal-planning rotation for the last few years and is also one of the favorites on my blog. The flavors are incredible and it can be made in half an hour in a single pan, making it a favorite for how clean my kitchen stays as well!

4 tablespoons (½ stick) unsalted butter

1 large onion

1 pound ground beef, venison, or bison

1 tablespoon curry powder

1 teaspoon sea salt

1 teaspoon freshly ground black pepper

1 teaspoon ground cinnamon

1 teaspoon ground ginger

1 teaspoon ground turmeric

1 teaspoon garlic powder

1 15-ounce can diced tomatoes

4 medium sweet potatoes

1 pound green beans

2 tablespoons Chicken Bone Broth (page 152) or store-bought or water

In a large skillet over medium heat, melt the butter. Dice the onion and add to the skillet. Sauté for 3 minutes, until the onion starts to become translucent. Add the beef, breaking it up, and cook until well browned, about 10 minutes. Stir in the curry powder, salt, pepper, cinnamon, ginger, turmeric, and garlic powder. Drain the tomatoes, peel and dice the sweet potatoes, and trim the green beans, then add all to the skillet.

Taste and adjust the seasonings if needed. Cover the skillet and simmer for 20 minutes, or until the sweet potatoes have softened. Check after 10 minutes and add a couple of tablespoons of broth if needed. Serve warm and enjoy!

chicken satay skewers

TOTAL TIME 2 hr. 25 min. (including marinade time) **ACTIVE TIME** 25 min. **SERVINGS** 6

This is a flavorful grilled chicken with satay flavors of honey, soy sauce, and curry. I often make this recipe on busy nights, because it comes together so quickly!

Zest and juice of 1 organic lime

2 tablespoons fish sauce

2 tablespoons honey

2 tablespoons coconut aminos or wheat-free fermented soy sauce

½ teaspoon curry powder

1 teaspoon garlic powder

½ teaspoon salt

1 teaspoon freshly ground black pepper

1 pound skinless, boneless chicken breasts or thighs

1 batch Satay Dipping Sauce (page 317) or peanut dipping sauce

In a small bowl, whisk together the lime zest and juice, fish sauce, honey, coconut aminos, curry powder, garlic powder, salt, and pepper.

Slice the chicken into roughly 1-inch-long strips against the grain. Place the chicken strips in a wide dish and pour the marinade over to coat. Cover and refrigerate for at least 2 hours, or preferably overnight.

Two hours before cooking, soak enough skewers for all of your chicken strips.

Preheat a grill pan or a grill to medium-high heat.

Place the chicken on the skewers and grill for 3 to 4 minutes per side, until cooked through. Serve with the dipping sauce.

tip: Marinate a day in advance if you have the time. This allows the flavors to intensify and also reduces prep time on the day you serve.

meatball-stuffed
spaghetti squash

TOTAL TIME 2 hr. | **ACTIVE TIME** 20 min. | **SERVINGS** 4

If prepared correctly, spaghetti squash is a delicious alternative to regular processed pastas, packing more nutrients and flavor. I love to bake meatballs and sauce directly in halves of spaghetti squash for premade spaghetti "bowls" that are delicious and fun for the kids!

2 spaghetti squash

¼ cup olive oil

1 pound ground beef

1 teaspoon garlic powder

1 teaspoon salt

½ teaspoon freshly ground black pepper

1 teaspoon Italian Seasoning (page 298) or store-bought

4 ounces fresh spinach

1 onion

½ cup grated Parmesan cheese (optional)

2 cups Easy Marinara Sauce from Fresh Tomatoes (page 319) or store-bought

1 cup shredded mozzarella cheese (optional)

Preheat the oven to 375°F.

Cut the spaghetti squash in half lengthwise and scoop out the seeds and discard. Drizzle each squash half with oil and place facedown on a baking sheet. Bake for about 30 minutes, until the squash is starting to get tender (but is not completely soft).

While the squash is baking, place the ground beef in a large bowl. Add the garlic powder, salt, pepper, and Italian seasoning. Finely mince the spinach and finely chop the onion and add both to the bowl. Add the Parmesan cheese, if using. Mix the beef mixture by hand until well combined and form into 1-inch meatballs. Place on a large plate or flat baking dish.

Remove the squash from the oven and turn the halves cut side up.

Evenly distribute the meatballs among the squash halves and then evenly pour the marinara sauce over them. Return to the oven for another 30 to 45 minutes, until the meatballs are cooked through and no longer pink in the middle. Top with the mozzarella cheese, if using. Serve each spaghetti squash half as a serving (halve as needed for children). To eat, use a fork to loosen the spaghetti squash from the sides of the "bowl" and eat like spaghetti.

sriracha shrimp
lettuce wraps

TOTAL TIME 20 min. | ACTIVE TIME 10 min. | SERVINGS 4

Sriracha is a delicious hot sauce with the usual hot notes and a subtle sweetness as well. Though its history is debated, it is generally said to have originated in Thailand and is named after a city there: Si Racha. Now it is a trendy condiment and is often used in sushi and other dishes. I like it with shrimp in this simple recipe.

1 tablespoon coconut oil

1 pound shrimp, peeled, tails removed, and deveined

¼ cup sriracha sauce

½ teaspoon garlic powder

1 head of Bibb or similar lettuce to get 8 large leaves

1 lime

Sour cream (optional)

Heat the oil in a medium saucepan over medium heat. Add the shrimp and sriracha. Sprinkle with the garlic powder and sauté for about 8 minutes, until the shrimp are cooked and the sauce has started to thicken. Let cool slightly.

Wash, dry, and separate the lettuce leaves. Fill each with ⅛ of the sriracha shrimp. Cut the lime into wedges and squeeze over the shrimp in the lettuce. Top with sour cream, if using, and fold the leaves over to wrap.

chicken tetrazzini

TOTAL TIME 1 hr.   **ACTIVE TIME** 30 min.   **SERVINGS** 4

Don't let the name confuse you: Though it sounds Italian, this is an American dish. No matter where it originated, the flavors are delicious and I love this creamy chicken-mushroom recipe served over zucchini noodles.

4 medium zucchini

¼ cup olive oil

1 pound skinless, boneless chicken breasts

1 teaspoon salt

1 teaspoon freshly ground black pepper

1 pound portabello mushrooms

1 yellow onion

4 garlic cloves

½ cup dry white wine

1 tablespoon minced fresh thyme

1 cup heavy cream or Coconut Milk (page 278)

1 tablespoon arrowroot powder

1 cup frozen peas

Preheat the oven to 400°F.

Peel the zucchini and use a spiralizer to create noodles. Set aside on a clean towel.

Heat the oil in a large ovenproof skillet over medium heat.

Cut the chicken into bite-size pieces and add to the skillet. Sprinkle with the salt and pepper and sauté for 10 to 14 minutes, until the chicken is opaque and no longer pink in the middle. Remove the chicken from the skillet and set aside.

Slice the mushrooms and add to the skillet. Sauté for 2 minutes. Add more oil if needed. Thinly slice the onion and mince the garlic and add both to the skillet. Sauté for 3 to 4 minutes, until the onion is translucent.

Add the wine (or substitute with white wine vinegar) to deglaze the skillet and sauté an additional 2 to 3 minutes, until the wine evaporates. Sprinkle the thyme into the skillet and add the cream and arrowroot, stirring until the sauce thickens, about 2 minutes. Add more arrowroot if needed to thicken. Stir in the frozen peas until just warmed. Return the chicken to the skillet and add the zucchini noodles. Toss well to coat evenly.

Place the skillet in the oven and bake for 25 to 30 minutes, until the zucchini noodles have softened.

tip: For a great topping, mix 1 cup almond flour, 4 tablespoons melted butter, and 1 cup Parmesan cheese. Sprinkle over the mixture before baking for a delicious crust. Garnish with chopped fresh parsley, if desired.

mongolian beef

TOTAL TIME 20 min. | ACTIVE TIME 20 min. | SERVINGS 4

I cringe to think that this was one of my staple foods in college, and not a homemade version. I'd grab some to go at the local restaurant near campus and I didn't realize until I started looking at recipes and trying to make my own how much refined sugar is added! I now make this much more healthful version with maple syrup and fresh spices, and my family loves it!

1 cup plus 2 tablespoons coconut oil

1 tablespoon minced fresh garlic

1 tablespoon minced peeled fresh ginger

½ cup wheat-free fermented soy sauce or coconut aminos

¾ cup pure maple syrup

2 pounds flank steak or other similar cut of beef

3 tablespoons arrowroot powder or cornstarch

3 green onions, thinly sliced on the diagonal

Melt 2 tablespoons oil in a large skillet or wok over high heat. Add the garlic and ginger and sauté over medium heat until fragrant, 2 to 3 minutes. Add the soy sauce and maple syrup and stir for 1 to 2 minutes, until the flavors incorporate. Remove from the heat and let cool. When cooled, pour the sauce into a small bowl and set aside. Wipe any residue out of the skillet.

Thinly slice the steak against the grain into ¼-inch slices. Dust the beef slices with the arrowroot to coat and let sit for about 5 minutes.

Heat 1 cup of oil in the same large skillet used for the sauce over medium-high heat. Add the beef and cook for 3 to 4 minutes, until the edges start to darken. Remove from the heat and set the steak aside on a paper-towel-lined plate to drain. Pour the excess oil from the skillet into a heat-safe container. Reduce the heat to medium and return the steak to the skillet.

Pour in the sauce and simmer for 1 to 2 minutes, until the sauce barely starts to thicken and the beef is well coated. Sprinkle the green onions over the top of the steak and serve.

halibut with lemon-butter sauce

TOTAL TIME 20 min.　　**ACTIVE TIME** 20 min.　　**SERVINGS** 4

Delicious halibut lightly marinated and served with a butter, wine, and lemon sauce tastes like it came from a fancy restaurant, but you can whip it up at home in just minutes.

Juice of 1 lemon

¼ cup olive oil

1 teaspoon salt

1 teaspoon freshly ground black pepper

2 finely minced garlic cloves or 1 teaspoon garlic powder

4 halibut fillets, skinned and deboned (4 ounces each)

8 tablespoons (1 stick) unsalted butter, at room temperature

Zest and juice of 1 organic lemon

¼ cup minced fresh parsley

¼ cup dry white wine (optional)

In a medium bowl, whisk together the juice of 1 lemon, the oil, salt, pepper, and garlic. Add the fish to the marinade bowl, cover, and place in the refrigerator for at least 30 minutes or up to overnight.

In a small bowl, use a fork to mash together 4 tablespoons of the butter, the zest and juice of 1 lemon, the parsley, and white wine, if using. This will create a thick sauce.

In a large skillet over medium heat, melt the remaining 4 tablespoons butter. Remove the fish from the marinade, allowing the excess sauce to drip off. Place the fish in the skillet and cook approximately 5 minutes per side, until cooked through and it flakes easily when pulled with a fork. Remove from the heat and top with a scoop of the lemon-butter mixture. Serve immediately.

chicken diane

TOTAL TIME 25 min.   ACTIVE TIME 15 min.   SERVINGS 4

Delicious chicken flavored with simple spices and served with mushrooms makes a delicious dinner in less than half an hour.

1 pound skinless, boneless chicken breasts

1 teaspoon salt

1 teaspoon freshly ground black pepper

1 teaspoon garlic powder

¼ cup coconut or olive oil

3 cups white mushrooms, sliced

Juice of 1 lime

½ cup Chicken Bone Broth (page 152) or store-bought

2 tablespoons finely minced fresh chives

3 tablespoons finely minced fresh parsley

1 teaspoon Dijon mustard

Cut the chicken breasts in half lengthwise and flatten by pounding with a meat hammer or the bottom of a cast-iron skillet until about ¼ to ½ inch thick. Sprinkle the chicken halves with the salt, pepper, and garlic powder.

Heat the oil in a large skillet over medium-high heat. Add the chicken and cook for 4 to 6 minutes per side, until opaque white and no longer pink in the middle. Remove the chicken from the skillet.

Add the mushrooms and sauté until browned. Add the lime juice, broth, chives, parsley, and mustard and whisk to combine. Simmer for 2 to 3 minutes, until the flavors are incorporated. Serve the chicken with the broth-and-herb sauce.

sloppy joe sweet potatoes

TOTAL TIME 1 hr. | **ACTIVE TIME** 10 min. | **SERVINGS** 4

Sloppy joes are a classic "kid" food, but I absolutely despised and dreaded them as a kid! I always thought that they were cloyingly sweet and that the flavor was off. At the same time, they are simple to make and a good starter recipe for kids who want to help in the kitchen. We experimented, and our favorite version gets just a hint of natural sweetness from the sweet potato "bun" it is served in.

4 medium sweet potatoes

1 pound ground beef

1 bell pepper, cored, seeded, and finely diced

1 small onion, finely diced

1 cup Homemade Ketchup (page 315) or store-bought

1 teaspoon garlic powder

2 tablespoons pure maple syrup

1 tablespoon chili powder (see Note, page 297)

½ teaspoon salt

½ teaspoon freshly ground black pepper

Preheat the oven to 375°F. Place the sweet potatoes on a baking sheet and bake for 45 minutes or until soft.

In a large skillet over medium heat, brown the beef, breaking it up as it cooks, about 10 minutes. Add the bell pepper, onion, ketchup, garlic powder, maple syrup, chili powder, salt, and pepper to the skillet. Stir in ½ cup water. Sauté over medium heat for 15 minutes, or until the onion and pepper have softened and the sauce has thickened. Remove from the heat and let cool slightly.

Remove the sweet potatoes from the oven. When cool enough to handle, slice the potatoes lengthwise and top with the beef mixture. Serve immediately.

sesame chicken
with sugar snap peas

TOTAL TIME 30 min.	ACTIVE TIME 30 min.	SERVINGS 4

Sesame chicken was another take-out favorite I once loved but was shocked to find out what the ingredients were once I started trying to re-create the recipe! My version uses a natural marinade with rice vinegar and coconut aminos and fresh ginger to achieve the same flavor without additives or sugar.

2 tablespoons toasted sesame oil

2 pounds skinless, boneless chicken breasts or thighs

½ cup Chicken Bone Broth (page 152) or store-bought

1 tablespoon finely minced peeled ginger

1 teaspoon garlic powder

1 teaspoon salt

1 teaspoon freshly ground black pepper

½ pound sugar snap peas

¼ cup coconut aminos or wheat-free fermented soy sauce

2 tablespoons rice vinegar

½ cup honey

¼ cup sesame seeds, toasted

Heat the oil in a large skillet or wok over medium-high heat. Thinly slice the chicken and add to the skillet. Add the broth and ginger and sprinkle with the garlic powder, salt, and pepper.

Cook for 8 to 10 minutes, until the chicken is almost cooked through. Add the sugar snaps and cook an additional 2 to 3 minutes, until tender, and the chicken is opaque white and not pink in the middle.

In a small bowl, whisk together the coconut aminos, vinegar, and honey. Add to the skillet and cook until the flavors are incorporated and the sauce starts to thicken. Remove from the heat, sprinkle with the sesame seeds, and serve.

simple salmon chowder

TOTAL TIME 25 min. | **ACTIVE TIME** 25 min. | **SERVINGS** 4

A 25-minute budget-friendly soup that uses cauliflower and canned salmon, this is a favorite at our house in the cooler months.

4 slices bacon

1 onion

3 stalks celery

1 head cauliflower

4 cups Chicken Bone Broth (page 152) or store-bought

1 15-ounce can salmon, with juice

2 teaspoons dried dill

1 teaspoon dried thyme

1 teaspoon salt

1 teaspoon freshly ground black pepper

2 cups Coconut Milk (page 278) or heavy cream

1 bunch of green onions (optional)

In a large soup pot over medium-high heat, cook the bacon until browned. Remove with tongs to a paper-towel-lined plate to drain. Leave the grease in the pot to sauté the vegetables in.

Dice the onion and celery, add to the pot, and sauté for 2 minutes, or until the vegetables start to soften. Break the cauliflower into medium-size florets and add to the pot. Pour in the broth and bring to a simmer. Simmer for 5 to 7 minutes, until the cauliflower has softened. Add the salmon and its juices, the dill, thyme, salt, and pepper and simmer for 5 minutes to warm through.

Pour in the coconut milk and bring to a simmer for 2 to 3 minutes to incorporate the flavors. Thinly slice the green onions, if using. Rough chop the bacon. Remove the chowder from the heat, divide among four bowls, garnish with the green onions and bacon, and serve.

savory seafood bisque

TOTAL TIME 45 min. | **ACTIVE TIME** 15 min. | **SERVINGS** 4

Once a month, my husband and I go on an actual date and often end up at our favorite local restaurant for one reason: seafood bisque. This soup is so good that often it's all we'll order. I re-created a budget-friendly version so we could make it a regular family meal.

4 tablespoons (½ stick) unsalted butter

1 shallot, finely chopped

4 garlic cloves, finely minced

2 tablespoons grated carrots

1 stalk celery, finely chopped

¼ cup dry wine (optional)

2 cups Chicken Bone Broth (page 152) or store-bought

1 teaspoon salt

½ teaspoon white pepper

1 teaspoon paprika (see Note, page 297)

½ teaspoon dried thyme

2 large lobsters or 1 cup lump lobster

2 6.5-ounce cans clams, minced, with juice

1 cup lump crab meat

2 cups heavy cream

In a large soup pot over medium heat, melt the butter, then add the shallot, garlic, carrots, and celery. Sauté the vegetables until tender, 10 to 12 minutes. Add the wine, if using, to deglaze and cook 30 seconds, until it has evaporated. Stir in the broth, salt, pepper, paprika, and thyme. Puree with an immersion blender until completely smooth. Bring the soup to a boil and add the lobsters. You may need to cook one at a time depending on the liquid level. Boil for 6 minutes, until the lobsters are bright red, and remove immediately with tongs.

When cool enough, separate the meat from the shell. Chop the meat and return to the pot. (If you're using lump lobster, just stir into the pot.) Add the clams and their juice and the crabmeat and cook until just hot, about 2 to 3 minutes. Stir in the heavy cream and simmer until thickened, about 4 minutes. Serve immediately, or for better flavor, cover and refrigerate overnight and reheat slowly before serving.

ground beef–vegetable soup

TOTAL TIME 1 hr.   ACTIVE TIME 15 min.   SERVINGS 4

This budget-friendly beef and vegetable soup is almost as easy as opening a can and so much more delicious! It uses ground beef as an inexpensive option that pairs well with the vegetables and spices in this recipe. If you make it ahead and store in the freezer, just thaw and reheat it for a quick weeknight meal.

2 pounds ground beef, preferably grass-fed

1 onion

4 stalks celery

4 medium carrots

2 tablespoons unsalted butter or coconut oil

1 pound fresh or frozen green beans, cut into 1-inch pieces

1 pound butternut squash or sweet potatoes, cut into ½-inch cubes

1 15-ounce can tomato sauce

1 14.5-ounce can diced tomatoes

1 teaspoon salt

1 teaspoon freshly ground black pepper

2 tablespoons Italian Seasoning (page 298) or store-bought

2 cups Beef Bone Broth (page 154) or store-bought

1 teaspoon garlic powder

In a large soup pot over medium heat, brown the beef, breaking it up as it cooks, until completely browned. Remove the beef to a paper-towel-lined plate to drain. Finely chop the onion, celery, and carrots and add to the pot along with the butter and sauté for 4 minutes, until the vegetables start to soften. Add the remaining ingredients and the beef, and bring to a boil. Reduce the heat and simmer for 45 minutes, or until all the vegetables are cooked and soft. Serve immediately.

creamy broccoli soup
(with extra veggies)

TOTAL TIME 30 min. | **ACTIVE TIME** 10 min. | **SERVINGS** 6

Canned "cream of" soups are often used in recipes or even eaten alone, but I always found it suspect that "cream" isn't high up on the ingredient list (or even present at all in some cases!). My homemade versions use high-quality real ingredients for nourishing, satisfying soups.

4 tablespoons (½ stick) unsalted butter or ¼ cup coconut oil

2 pounds fresh broccoli

1 leek

1 onion

1 carrot

4 garlic cloves

1 teaspoon salt

1 teaspoon freshly ground black pepper

½ teaspoon celery salt

4 cups Chicken Bone Broth (page 152) or store-bought

½ cup heavy cream (optional)

8 ounces Cheddar cheese, grated (optional)

In a large soup pot over medium-high heat, melt the butter. Cut the florets off the broccoli stalks and add to the pot. With a paring knife, carefully peel the stalks, chop them into small pieces, and add to the pot. Remove the outer layer of the leek and cut off the root and the thick part of the green stem. Wash well, then thinly slice and add to the pot. Dice the onion, chop the carrot, and smash the garlic and add all to the pot. Season with the salt, pepper, and celery salt.

Sauté until the vegetables are tender and the onion is translucent and just starting to brown, 5 minutes. Pour in the broth, bring to a boil, then reduce the heat to a simmer. Simmer for 20 minutes, or until all the vegetables are tender. Puree with an immersion blender until smooth. Add the cream, if using, and blend. Serve hot, topped with the cheese, if desired.

tip: Serve alone or add precooked leftover chicken, beef, or sausage for a full meal!

simple miso soup

TOTAL TIME 10 min. | **ACTIVE TIME** 10 min. | **SERVINGS** 4

A staple first course at many Japanese restaurants, miso soup is one of the easiest soups to make at home and a great base for many other types of soup. This is the first soup that our kids learned to prepare and we often serve this with a stir-fry or salad.

2 teaspoons dashi granules

2 quarts Chicken Bone Broth (page 152) or store-bought or water

¼ cup miso paste

2 tablespoons light miso paste

3 green onions, thinly sliced

In a large saucepan, combine the dashi granules and the broth and bring to a boil. Reduce the heat to medium-low and whisk or blend in both miso pastes. Simmer for 3 to 4 minutes, remove from the heat, and divide among four bowls.

Just before serving, garnish each bowl with a scattering of the green onions.

tip: Add some chopped leftover protein like chicken or fish to make this a full meal!

chicken pot pie soup

TOTAL TIME 30 min. | **ACTIVE TIME** 10 min. | **SERVINGS** 4

Chicken pot pie is a delicious but somewhat time-consuming classic meal. In the winter, I prefer to take the same ingredients and flavors and make a delicious soup instead. Not only does this save time (and dishes), but it accomplishes the same flavor without the need for a crust!

4 tablespoons (½ stick) unsalted butter

1 pound skinless, boneless chicken breasts

4 carrots

4 celery ribs

1 onion

3 organic Yukon Gold potatoes, peeled

4 cups Chicken Bone Broth (page 152) or store-bought

1 cup Coconut Milk (page 278)

1 teaspoon salt

½ teaspoon freshly ground black pepper

1 teaspoon garlic powder

½ teaspoon dried thyme

1 10-ounce package frozen peas

2 tablespoons arrowroot powder

In a large soup pot over medium-high heat, melt the butter. Chop the chicken into ½-inch or smaller cubes and add to the pot. Cook for 5 to 7 minutes, until the chicken is white on all sides. Remove the chicken from the pot and set aside.

Chop the carrots, celery, onion, and potatoes and place in the pot. Sauté for 5 minutes, or until the vegetables start to soften. Stir in the broth and coconut milk. Add the salt, pepper, garlic powder, and thyme.

Simmer for 10 minutes, or until all the vegetables have softened. Return the chicken to the pot and add the peas. Simmer for 2 to 3 more minutes, until the chicken is completely cooked through and not pink in the middle.

Sprinkle the arrowroot into the pot and allow the broth to thicken slightly. Coconut Flour Biscuits (page 55) are a nice accompaniment.

oyster stew

It seems there are two types of people in the world: those who absolutely love oysters in any form and those who don't understand how anyone could eat an oyster in any form. I fall firmly in the first group and if you are a card-carrying member of the latter, this may not be a recipe for you. At the same time, this is one of the few recipes that seems to be able to toe the line between groups and I have high hopes that it may one day end the oyster wars altogether!

4 tablespoons (½ stick) butter

24 ounces oysters, shucked, liquid reserved

3 stalks celery

2 shallots

1 cup milk

1 teaspoon salt

1 teaspoon white pepper

¼ teaspoon ground cayenne pepper

1 teaspoon paprika (see Note, page 297)

½ teaspoon garlic powder

1 cup heavy cream

3 green onions

In a large skillet over medium heat, melt the butter. Add the oysters and heat for 3 to 4 minutes, until the edges just start to curl. Remove the oysters and set aside.

Finely dice the celery and shallots and add to the pan. Sauté for 10 minutes, or until soft.

Add the milk and bring to a simmer. Puree with an immersion blender until smooth. Stir in the salt, pepper, cayenne, paprika, and garlic powder.

Return the oysters to the pan and add the oyster liquid. Simmer for another 3 to 4 minutes, until the flavors incorporate. Stir in the heavy cream until just heated. Very thinly slice the green onions and add to the pan. Remove from the heat and serve.

marcie's moroccan chicken stir-fry

TOTAL TIME 30 min. | **ACTIVE TIME** 10 min. | **SERVINGS** 4

Who would think to put broccoli, garam masala, raisins, and olives together? Definitely not me . . . until a friend made me this stir-fry right after I had a baby and I fell in love with the flavor. I asked her for the recipe and adapted it slightly to suit our taste preferences. We love this simple staple stir-fry with big flavor.

2 tablespoons coconut oil or unsalted butter

4 skinless, boneless chicken breasts or thighs (about 2 pounds)

4 large carrots

1 onion

1 head of broccoli

1 tablespoon garam masala

¼ cup Chicken Bone Broth (page 152) or store-bought or water

Sea salt and freshly ground black pepper to taste

¼ cup raisins (optional)

½ cup green olives (optional)

Heat the oil in a large soup pot over medium-high heat. Chop the chicken into bite-size pieces and sauté until cooked, 7 to 9 minutes. Slice the carrots and onion very thinly, add to the pot, and cook for 5 minutes, or until the vegetables start to soften. Cut the broccoli into small florets, add to the pot, and sauté for another 3 to 4 minutes.

Add the garam masala and broth and simmer for 5 minutes, or until all the vegetables are tender. Season with salt and pepper to taste. Remove from the heat, divide among four bowls, and top each bowl with some raisins and green olives, if using.

caramelized french onion meat loaf

TOTAL TIME 1 hr. 20 min. | **ACTIVE TIME** 30 min. | **SERVINGS** 4

Meat loaf is a timeless classic, but many recipes call for canned or packaged soups or other processed ingredients. Up the nutrition and the flavor by using slowly caramelized onions instead, and this recipe is sure to become a family favorite!

2 pounds ground beef or bison

¾ cup almond flour

2 eggs

½ cup Homemade Ketchup (page 315) or store-bought

1 teaspoon salt

1 teaspoon garlic powder

1 teaspoon white pepper

2 tablespoons coconut oil

3 large sweet onions

2 tablespoons pure maple syrup

½ teaspoon celery salt

2 tablespoons dry red wine

Preheat the oven to 350°F.

Place the beef, flour, eggs, ketchup, salt, garlic powder, and pepper in a large bowl and mix by hand until combined. Set aside.

Heat the oil in a large skillet over medium heat. Thinly slice the onions and add to the skillet. Sauté, stirring occasionally, 15 to 18 minutes, until caramelized and completely soft. Stir in the maple syrup and celery salt. Raise the heat to high for 1 minute, or until the onions just start to crackle. Immediately add the wine to deglaze the skillet and remove from the heat.

Blend the onion mixture with an immersion blender until smooth. Pour the onion mixture into the meat bowl and stir to combine. Shape the meat into a loaf and place in the middle of a 9 × 13-inch baking pan.

Bake the meat loaf, uncovered, for 45 to 60 minutes, until browned and the internal temperature reads 160°F. Remove from the oven, let cool 10 minutes, then slice and serve.

184 the wellness mama cookbook

chicken egg drop soup

TOTAL TIME 1 hr.   ACTIVE TIME 20 min.   SERVINGS 4

Egg drop soup is simple to prepare, and adding chicken gives this basic recipe an extra boost of protein and flavor and makes it a full meal!

1 4-pound chicken

2 onions

8 carrots

4 stalks celery

1 teaspoon curry powder, or to taste

1 teaspoon garlic salt, or to taste

1 teaspoon freshly ground black pepper, or to taste

4 large eggs

Fill a large pot with water and bring to a boil. Boil the chicken until it reaches an internal temperature of 180°F, about 45 minutes. Remove the chicken, but leave the liquid in the pot.

When cool enough to handle, separate the chicken from the bones and chop the chicken into bite-size pieces. (Reserve the bones for making broth.) Chop the onions, carrots, and celery and add all to the pot. Bring to a boil and let the vegetables soften, about 10 minutes. Add the chopped chicken back in and season with the curry powder, garlic salt, and pepper.

Reduce the heat to a simmer, break the eggs into the pot, and stir vigorously. Simmer until the eggs are cooked, about 2 minutes, and remove from the heat. Serve and enjoy.

slow cooker
simplicity

If you can't feed a hundred people, then feed just one.

—MOTHER TERESA

CHICKEN

DO NOT PUT CROCK OR B...

Questions? Call
www.cro...

italian red pepper pot roast

TOTAL TIME 8 hr. 10 min.   **ACTIVE TIME** 10 min.   **SERVINGS** 8+

Savory red peppers and artichokes unite with garlic to make this complex-tasting yet easy-to-prepare pot roast! Serve over zucchini or parsnip "noodles" sautéed in olive oil for a simple meal on a busy day.

1 3-pound chuck roast

1 jar roasted red peppers

1 jar marinated artichoke hearts

1 medium onion

8 garlic cloves

1 cup Beef Bone Broth (page 154) or store-bought

2 tablespoons Italian Seasoning (page 298) or store-bought

Place the roast in a 6-quart slow cooker. Drain the red peppers and artichokes, slice the onion into ¼-inch slices, and smash the garlic, then add all to the slow cooker. Pour in the broth and add the Italian seasoning. Turn the slow cooker on low for at least 8 hours, or until the meat is fork tender. When done, remove the roast to a serving platter. Strain the fat off the remaining liquid with a large spoon.

Place all of the vegetables and 1 cup of the remaining liquid in a blender and blend on high until smooth to make an Italian-style gravy. Pour the gravy over the roast to serve. Store leftovers in the refrigerator for up to 4 days with the remaining gravy and the flavors will intensify with time.

tip: Serve over rice, roasted cabbage, or vegetable noodles.

mississippi pot roast

TOTAL TIME 8 hr. 10 min. ┊ **ACTIVE TIME** 10 min. ┊ **SERVINGS** 8+

Though I lived in Mississippi for years, I never discovered this delicious pot roast variation until I moved out of the state. Many recipes call for cream-based canned soups, but this version has more flavor with fresh onions, spices, and pepperoncini!

1 4- to 5-pound chuck roast

1 tablespoon dried dill

1 teaspoon garlic powder

1 tablespoon onion powder (see Note, page 297)

1 teaspoon salt

1 teaspoon freshly ground black pepper

½ teaspoon celery salt (optional)

1 onion

4 tablespoons (½ stick) unsalted butter

1 cup Beef Bone Broth (page 154) or store-bought

¼ cup coconut aminos or wheat-free fermented soy sauce

1 16-ounce jar pepperoncini

Place the roast in a 6-quart slow cooker. Sprinkle with the dill, garlic powder, onion powder, salt, pepper, and celery salt, if using. Slice the onion and add it and the butter to the slow cooker.

Pour the broth and coconut aminos over the meat. Arrange the pepperoncini over the meat. Turn on the slow cooker and cook on low for at least 8 hours, until the meat is tender. Use two forks to gently shred the beef before serving.

meatballs in marinara

TOTAL TIME 8 hr. 20 min. | ACTIVE TIME 20 min. | SERVINGS 8+

Meatballs can be messy and time consuming to prepare, but I've found that making them in the slow cooker is the perfect solution and we get to look forward to dinner all day as the flavors intensify and fill the air in our house!

2 pounds ground beef

1 cup almond flour or bread crumbs

3 eggs

¼ cup grated Parmesan cheese (optional)

1 tablespoon Italian Seasoning (page 298) or store-bought

1 teaspoon salt

1 teaspoon freshly ground black pepper

1 teaspoon garlic powder

2 medium onions

4 garlic cloves

1 28-ounce can crushed tomatoes, drained

2 15-ounce cans tomato sauce

1 6-ounce can tomato paste

Place the ground beef, flour, eggs, Parmesan, if using, Italian seasoning, salt, pepper, and garlic powder in a medium bowl. Mix well with your hands and form into 1-inch meatballs. Carefully place these in the slow cooker. Finely chop the onions, smash the garlic, and sprinkle both over the meatballs. Pour in the crushed tomatoes and tomato sauce, then add the tomato paste. (The tomato paste is thick, but it will incorporate nicely as everything cooks.)

Cook on low for 6 to 8 hours, or on high for 4 hours. Halfway through the cooking process, gently stir the sauce and flip the meatballs to ensure that they cook evenly. Serve alone or over spaghetti squash or pasta noodles.

soulful bbq ribs

TOTAL TIME 6 hr.　ACTIVE TIME 10 min.　SERVINGS 6+

I've never had great luck making ribs on a grill. They end up too dry or too tough, but I can make some mean ribs in a slow cooker. Cheating? Maybe, but I don't care!

1 medium onion

4 pounds beef ribs

1 teaspoon chili powder
(see Note, page 297)

1 teaspoon garlic powder

Sea salt

Freshly ground black pepper

1 15-ounce can tomato sauce

1 6-ounce can tomato paste

2 tablespoons apple cider
vinegar

2 tablespoons Worcestershire
sauce

¼ cup molasses, preferably
blackstrap

¼ cup honey

Finely dice the onion and place in a 6-quart slow cooker. Cut every 3 to 4 ribs, season the ribs with the chili powder, garlic powder, salt, and pepper, and place on top of the onion.

In a medium bowl, whisk together the tomato sauce, tomato paste, vinegar, Worcestershire sauce, molasses, and honey, then pour evenly over the ribs. Cover and cook on low for 6 to 8 hours, until the meat is tender and pulls apart easily.

slow cooker boston butt

| TOTAL TIME 10 hr. | ACTIVE TIME 5 min. | SERVINGS 4 |

Here's a classic barbecue favorite made in the slow cooker. When cooked slowly, Boston butt becomes amazingly tender and flavorful, and this mixture of spices, pineapple, and barbecue sauce completes the dish.

2 large sweet onions

5 pounds Boston butt roast

1 tablespoon chili powder (see Note, page 297)

1 tablespoon paprika (see Note, page 297)

1 tablespoon garlic powder

1 tablespoon dried basil

1 tablespoon celery salt

1 tablespoon sea salt

1 teaspoon freshly ground black pepper

2 cups thinly chopped fresh pineapple or 1 15-ounce can crushed pineapple, with juice

2 cups BBQ Sauce (page 326)

Thinly slice the onions and place in a 6-quart or larger slow cooker. Rinse the meat and place on top of the onions. Add the chili powder, paprika, garlic powder, basil, celery salt, sea salt, pepper, and pineapple over it. Cook on low for 10 to 12 hours, until fork tender.

You can begin checking for tenderness at the 8-hour mark. Shred with two forks to make pulled pork and top with the barbecue sauce.

tip: Let this recipe cook overnight for use in BBQ sandwiches for lunch. If you're feeling really fancy, brown the meat on the grill or under the broiler when it is finished cooking and thicken the remaining sauce in the slow cooker to use as a topping.

ginger-orange glazed roast

TOTAL TIME 8 hr. 10 min.   **ACTIVE TIME** 10 min.   **SERVINGS** 8+

Ginger and orange are a match made in culinary heaven, and they combine in this delicious slow cooker recipe for a slightly sweet and very flavorful roast. I often start this in the slow cooker in the morning and it is ready to serve when the kids get hungry for dinner. This is great with Zucchini & Summer Squash Gratin (page 119).

4 pounds chuck or other type of roast

1 cup orange marmalade or Sicilian orange spread (no sugar added)

1 large onion

1 1-inch piece fresh ginger

¼ cup rice vinegar

1 cup Beef Bone Broth (page 154) or store-bought

2 tablespoons coconut aminos or wheat-free fermented soy sauce

1 teaspoon garlic powder

1 teaspoon freshly ground black pepper

1 teaspoon salt

¼ teaspoon ground cloves

Place the roast in a slow cooker and spread the marmalade evenly on top of the roast. Slice the onion and peel and chop the ginger. Add both to the slow cooker. Add the vinegar, broth, coconut aminos, garlic powder, pepper, salt, and cloves. Cook on low for at least 8 hours, until the meat is fork tender.

Remove from the heat and serve. (I like to serve it over rice and with a side of steamed broccoli.)

luck-of-the-irish corned beef & cabbage

TOTAL TIME 8 hr. | **ACTIVE TIME** 15 min. | **SERVINGS** 4

I'm Irish and French. My husband is Italian and German. This has made for an interesting combination of traditions on many holidays, but one holiday that I claim 100 percent without opposition is St. Patrick's Day, when we serve this classic corned beef and cabbage.

1 onion

3 carrots

1 stalk celery

1 3- to 4-pound corned beef brisket (recipe follows)

2 garlic cloves

1 tablespoon pickling spice

1 large head of cabbage

for the meat

5 garlic cloves, crushed, or ½ teaspoon garlic powder

1 cup Himalayan or other sea salt

½ cup raw cane sugar or brown sugar

1 cinnamon stick or ¼ teaspoon ground

1 tablespoon mustard seeds

1 to 2 tablespoons black peppercorns

1 tablespoon coriander seeds (optional)

1 teaspoon allspice berries (optional)

1 teaspoon juniper berries (optional)

½ teaspoon whole cloves

1 teaspoon minced peeled fresh ginger or ½ teaspoon ground

½ teaspoon dried thyme

2 to 3 bay leaves, crushed

2 cups ice

1 3- to 4-pound beef brisket, preferably grass-fed

¼ cup beet juice or juice from homemade sauerkraut made with purple cabbage (optional)

Chop the onion, carrots, and celery and place in a 6-quart slow cooker. Place the corned beef brisket in the slow cooker with the fat side up. Mince the garlic and sprinkle it and the pickling spice on top. Add 2 cups water and cook on low for 7 hours, or on high for 3 hours, until the meat is almost cooked. About 1 hour before the beef is done, slice the cabbage and place over the beef and cook until the cabbage is tender, and serve.

To make the meat: Place 2 quarts water, the garlic, salt, sugar, cinnamon stick, mustard seeds, peppercorns, coriander seeds, if using, allspice berries, if using, juniper berries, if using, cloves, ginger, thyme, and bay leaves in a large pot over high heat, stirring frequently, until the sugar and salt dissolve. Cool the liquid with the ice, and place in the refrigerator until completely cooled and less than 60°F. It is very important that the brine be cold before it comes in contact with the meat.

The brining process will take 3 to 5 days. Either place the brisket in a 2-gallon bag and add the brine, or place the brisket in a large glass container with a lid and add the brine. Either way, you want the brisket to be completely submerged and surrounded with the brine. Add the beet juice, if using.

Place the meat in the refrigerator (if your meat is in a plastic bag, place the bag inside a dish or another holding container in case it leaks) and leave it there for at least 3 days but, if possible, up to 5 days. Every day, flip the meat over and stir the brine. After 3 to 5 days, remove the meat from the brine, rinse with cool water, and cook as you normally would a corned beef brisket.

slow cooker beef stew

TOTAL TIME 8 hr. 10 min. **ACTIVE TIME** 10 min. **SERVINGS** 8+

Classic beef stew with a twist! Sweet potatoes provide depth of flavor and a subtle sweetness to this classic meal.

2 pounds stew beef, cut into 1-inch or smaller cubes

5 carrots, cut into ½-inch pieces

2 pounds sweet potatoes, peeled and chopped into ½-inch cubes

1 stalk celery, chopped into ¼-inch pieces

1 teaspoon salt

1 teaspoon white or freshly ground black pepper

1 teaspoon garlic powder

1 teaspoon paprika (see Note, page 297) or ground cumin seed

2 cups Beef Bone Broth (page 154) or store-bought

Place all the ingredients in a 6-quart slow cooker. Cook on low for 8 to 10 hours, or on high for 5 to 6 hours, until the meat is fork tender and it pulls apart easily.

Store leftovers in an airtight container in the refrigerator for up to 4 days and reheat before serving.

pork carnitas

TOTAL TIME 5 hr. 10 min. | **ACTIVE TIME** 10 min. | **SERVINGS** 12+

Carnitas means "little meats" and that is a perfect description of this recipe. The pork is slow roasted with spices, garlic, and oranges and then shredded. This is typically served in tortillas but is also delicious over a salad or with rice and roasted vegetables.

5 pounds pork roast or boneless pork shoulder

1 tablespoon salt

1 teaspoon freshly ground black pepper

1 tablespoon ground cumin

1 tablespoon chili powder (see Note, page 297)

1 onion

8 garlic cloves

2 organic oranges

1 organic lime

1 tablespoon pure maple syrup (optional)

Wash and dry the pork. Rub the pork with the salt, pepper, cumin, and chili powder and place in a 6-quart slow cooker. Chop the onion, smash the garlic, and place both on top of the pork. Zest the oranges and lime and squeeze the orange and lime juice over the pork. Cook on low for 10 hours, or on high for 4 to 5 hours, until tender. Remove from the slow cooker and place on a cutting board. When the meat is cool enough to handle, shred it and set aside. Skim off the fat from the slow cooker juice and discard.

Heat a large skillet over medium heat. Add the pork and cook until it starts to get crispy on one side. Once you have crisped all the pork, remove from the skillet and set aside. Add the slow cooker juices to the skillet and simmer until slightly reduced, about 8 minutes. Remove from the heat and whisk in the maple syrup, if using. Serve alone or in tortillas of choice topped with chopped fresh cilantro, sour cream, grated cheese of choice, and a squeeze of fresh lime juice.

teriyaki chicken thighs

TOTAL TIME 8 hr. 10 min. | ACTIVE TIME 10 min. | SERVINGS 8

Easy-on-the-budget chicken thighs are the perfect base for this sweet and savory teriyaki recipe! Make in the morning and serve over rice and with a side of steamed broccoli for an easy dinner on a busy night.

2 pounds skinless, boneless chicken thighs

½ cup coconut aminos or wheat-free fermented soy sauce

¼ cup rice wine vinegar

¼ cup honey

1 15-ounce can crushed pineapple (no sugar added), with juice

1 teaspoon garlic powder

1 teaspoon salt

1 teaspoon freshly ground black pepper

1 1-inch piece fresh ginger

1 onion

2 tablespoons sesame seeds

Place the chicken in a 6-quart slow cooker. Stir together the coconut aminos, vinegar, and honey and pour over the chicken. Pour the canned pineapple and its juice over the chicken. Sprinkle in the garlic powder, salt, and pepper.

Peel and finely mince the ginger and finely chop the onion and sprinkle over the pineapple mixture. Cook on low for 8 hours, or on high for 4 hours, until the chicken is tender. Before serving, sprinkle with the sesame seeds.

sweet orange chicken

| TOTAL TIME 4 hr. 10 min. | ACTIVE TIME 10 min. | SERVINGS 6+ |

Fruit flavors are a perfect complement to chicken and certain other meat dishes, and this sweet orange slow cooker chicken is definitely a kid favorite at our house. It smells delicious as it cooks all day and is perfect with rice or cauliflower!

2 pounds chicken breast or thighs

1 cup orange marmalade or Sicilian orange spread (no sugar added)

¼ cup coconut aminos

1 tablespoon rice vinegar

1 teaspoon garlic powder

1 teaspoon salt

1 teaspoon sesame oil

½ teaspoon white pepper

1 teaspoon red chili flakes (optional)

3 stalks green onions (optional)

Place all the ingredients except the green onions in a 6-quart slow cooker and stir to combine. Cook on low for 3 to 4 hours, or on high for 1½ to 2 hours, or until the chicken is tender. Slice the green onions, if using, and sprinkle on top to garnish.

filipino adobo chicken

TOTAL TIME 8 hr. 10 min.   ACTIVE TIME 10 min.   SERVINGS 8

Adobo, from the Spanish word meaning "marinade" or "sauce," is a popular method of food preparation in the Philippines and is used to prepare meats and even vegetables and seafoods. I personally love the classic vinegar, garlic, and coconut aminos flavors over chicken in this slow cooker favorite.

2 pounds skinless, boneless chicken thighs

¼ cup rice wine vinegar

¼ cup coconut aminos or wheat-free fermented soy sauce

1 onion

6 garlic cloves

1 teaspoon salt

1 teaspoon freshly ground black pepper

½ cup Chicken Bone Broth (page 152) or store-bought

Place the chicken in a 6-quart slow cooker. Pour the vinegar and coconut aminos over the chicken. Finely chop the onion and mince the garlic and add both to the slow cooker. Season with the salt and pepper and pour in the broth. Cook on low for 5 to 6 hours, or on high for 2½ to 3 hours, until the chicken is tender. Serve over rice and with a vegetables side of your choice.

tip: To save time on a weeknight, combine all the ingredients in a storage container and place in the freezer. When ready to use, defrost overnight in the refrigerator, and in the morning pour the contents into the slow cooker and enjoy for dinner when you get home from work.

spinach-artichoke chicken

TOTAL TIME 4 hr.   **ACTIVE TIME** 10 min.   **SERVINGS** 4

Spinach-and-artichoke dip is one of my husband's favorite appetizers. The flavor combination is amazing and I've always felt that it was a shame to serve this delicious mixture of spinach, artichokes, and cheese alongside flavorless chips. At our house, we turn this "dip" into a full meal by serving it over chicken!

2 pounds skinless, boneless chicken breasts or strips

1 teaspoon garlic powder, or to taste

1 teaspoon sea salt, or to taste

½ teaspoon freshly ground black pepper, or to taste

1 10-ounce package frozen spinach

1 16-ounce jar marinated artichoke hearts

½ cup grated Parmesan cheese

8 ounces regular cream cheese

½ cup shredded mozzarella cheese (optional)

Chop the chicken into bite-size pieces and season with the garlic powder, salt, and pepper. Place in a 6-quart slow cooker and cook on low for 4 hours, or on high for 2 hours, until the chicken is cooked through and pulls apart easily.

One hour before the chicken is done, defrost and drain the spinach, squeezing out any excess liquid, and drain the artichoke hearts. Add the spinach, artichoke hearts, Parmesan cheese, and cream cheese to the slow cooker and cook for another hour until the cheeses are well melted. Stir to combine and incorporate the flavors. Top with the mozzarella cheese, if using, and serve.

restaurant-style slow
cooker fajita chicken

TOTAL TIME 8 hr. | **ACTIVE TIME** 5 min. | **SERVINGS** 4

Growing up, my go-to order at any Mexican restaurant was a chicken taco salad. We rarely eat out now, but I often re-create those flavors with this slow cooker fajita chicken base served under shredded lettuce, tomatoes, onions, guacamole, and other toppings!

4 skinless, boneless chicken breasts (about 2 pounds)

2 teaspoons onion powder (see Note, page 297)

2 teaspoons garlic powder

2 teaspoons sea salt

2 teaspoons freshly ground black pepper

2 teaspoons chili powder (see Note, page 297)

2 teaspoons ground cumin

1 onion

1 red bell pepper

1 green bell pepper

1 cup salsa of choice

Place the chicken in a 6-quart slow cooker and season with the onion powder, garlic powder, salt, pepper, chili powder, and cumin. Slice the onion and core, seed, and slice the bell peppers. Lay both the onion and pepper slices over the chicken. Pour the salsa over the chicken and vegetables. Cook on low for 7 to 8 hours, or on high for 2 to 3 hours.

When done, remove the chicken from the slow cooker, let cool slightly, and shred with two forks before serving. Serve over salad or with tacos.

tip: So many topping possibilities! Top with homemade guacamole (see page 223), sour cream, Frances's Red Hot Sauce (page 323), or grated cheese of choice, if desired.

bbq bacon-apple chicken

TOTAL TIME 8 hr. 10 min.   **ACTIVE TIME** 10 min.   **SERVINGS** 4

This is my son's favorite slow cooker recipe to make because it is so simple and because he absolutely loves barbecue. Apples add a hint of sweetness to the smoky barbecue flavor.

4 skinless, boneless chicken breasts or thighs (about 2 pounds)

8 slices bacon

2 apples

1 cup BBQ Sauce (page 326) or store-bought

1 teaspoon garlic powder

Wrap each piece of chicken in 2 pieces of bacon and place in a 6-quart slow cooker.

Peel, core, and grate the apples and place in a medium bowl. Add the barbecue sauce and mix, then pour over the chicken. Sprinkle with the garlic powder. Cook on low for 6 to 8 hours, or on high for 2 to 3 hours. Serve with sweet potatoes or coleslaw on the side.

light lunches

One of the very nicest things about life is the way
we must regularly stop whatever it is we are doing
and devote our attention to eating.

—LUCIANO PAVAROTTI

ground beef jerky

TOTAL TIME 12 hr. | ACTIVE TIME 10 min. | SERVINGS 4

Here is a budget-friendly variation of beef jerky using lean ground beef in place of beef steak. It's seasoned with simple salt, pepper, garlic, and coconut aminos, but you can mix up the flavors with a variety of spices.

Olive oil

3 pounds ground beef, venison, or bison

3 tablespoons Himalayan or other sea salt

1 tablespoon freshly ground black pepper (optional)

2 teaspoons garlic powder (see Note)

2 tablespoons coconut aminos

Preheat the oven to its lowest setting. (On my oven this is 170°F.) Lightly rub olive oil over a large baking sheet with a lip and set aside. (It is okay to use olive oil here because we aren't heating to high temps!)

Place the meat in a large bowl and season with the salt, pepper, and garlic powder. Using the side of a glass or a rolling pin, roll the meat evenly around the baking sheet to ¼-inch thickness. If it is too thick, use a second baking sheet. Using a butter knife, lightly score the meat to make the sizes you want for the jerky. (Alternatively, you can also skip this step and use kitchen scissors to cut into strips when the jerky's done.)

Brush the meat with the coconut aminos or fermented soy sauce if desired and sprinkle with a little extra sea salt. Place in the oven and bake for 8 to 12 hours, until hardened. Halfway through cooking, use a large spatula to flip the meat over. Cut it in half at this point if needed to flip. I usually stick this in at night and flip it in the morning—it's done a few hours later.

Store in an airtight container in the pantry for up to 2 weeks or keep in an airtight container in the freezer for up to 2 months.

note: You can use many flavor variations on this recipe: a Mexican flavor with cumin and cilantro; a Chinese variation with ginger and coconut aminos; or an Italian version with oregano, basil, marjoram, extra garlic powder, and pepper.

chipotle chicken fingers

TOTAL TIME 30 min. :: ACTIVE TIME 15 min. :: SERVINGS 4

Chicken fingers may be considered a kid-approved food (think about how many restaurant menus they appear on), but the traditional version with processed flour and vegetable oils is definitely not Mom approved in our house! I make a healthful variation of this childhood favorite by breading in almond flour and spices—and my kids love it. Serve with Honey Mustard (page 313).

3 skinless, boneless chicken breasts (about 2 pounds)

2 large eggs

1 teaspoon filtered water

1 cup almond flour

1 teaspoon garlic powder

1 teaspoon paprika (see Note, page 297)

1 teaspoon chili powder (see Note, page 297)

Sea salt and freshly ground black pepper

Coconut oil or tallow, for frying

1 cup Honey Mustard (page 313)

Preheat the oven to 200°F.

Cut the chicken into strips or nugget-size bites. In a medium bowl, beat the eggs with the water. Add the chicken strips and coat well.

On a large plate, mix the flour, garlic powder, paprika, chili powder, ½ teaspoon salt, and ½ teaspoon pepper.

Heat 1 inch of oil in a large skillet over medium-high heat. Once the oil is hot, take the chicken pieces out of the egg mixture and then dredge in the flour mixture and place in the skillet. Cook for 3 to 4 minutes per side, or until golden brown and no longer pink in the middle.

Remove from the skillet and place on a baking sheet in the oven to keep warm while the remaining batches are frying. When all the batches are done, sprinkle with salt and pepper and serve with the honey mustard on the side.

athena's greek meatballs

TOTAL TIME 55 min.   ACTIVE TIME 15 min.   SERVINGS 4

Named after my favorite goddess in Greek mythology, these meatballs combine delicious flavors of fennel, mint, citrus, and garlic with lean ground turkey and fresh Tzatziki Sauce (page 325) for a delicious meal any day of the week.

1 large onion

1 garlic clove

1 pound ground turkey or ground meat of choice

¼ cup almond flour, plus more if needed

2 large eggs

1 tablespoon chopped fennel bulb

1 tablespoon chopped fennel greens

Zest and juice of ½ organic lemon

1 teaspoon minced fresh mint

1 teaspoon garlic powder (see Note, page 297)

Sea salt to taste

Freshly ground black pepper to taste

1 batch Tzatziki Sauce (page 325)

Preheat the oven to 350°F. Oil a baking sheet or large baking dish and set aside.

Grate the onion into a large bowl. Mince the garlic and add to the bowl. Add the turkey, flour, eggs, chopped fennel bulb and greens, lemon zest and juice, mint, garlic powder, salt, and pepper and mix by hand. If necessary, add more flour, a tablespoon at a time, to make a thick enough mixture to form into meatballs.

Shape the mixture into 1-inch meatballs and place on the prepared baking sheet. Place in the oven for 30 to 40 minutes, or until cooked through and no longer pink in the middle. Serve the meatballs hot with tzatziki sauce on the side.

grain-free garlic-herb crackers

TOTAL TIME 20 min. | ACTIVE TIME 10 min. | SERVINGS 8

Crackers are a great base for easy snacks and meals. Just add cheese, hummus, guacamole, or other dips to make a filling and nourishing meal. Most crackers contain refined flours, sweeteners, and processed oils, but this homemade version has extra protein from almond flour and chia seeds and a subtle flavor from the onion and garlic powders.

2 tablespoons chia seeds

3 cups almond flour

1 teaspoon coconut flour

1 teaspoon salt

½ teaspoon freshly ground black pepper

½ teaspoon garlic powder (see Note, page 297)

½ teaspoon onion powder (see Note, page 297)

1 teaspoon dried parsley

2 large eggs

Preheat the oven to 350°F. Line a baking sheet with parchment paper and set aside.

Pulse the chia seeds in a food processor until powdered. Add the almond and coconut flours, salt, pepper, garlic powder, onion powder, and parsley and pulse to combine. Add the eggs and pulse until a stiff dough forms.

Divide the dough into two halves and roll each out between two pieces of parchment paper until very thin (under ⅛ inch). Cut into 1-inch squares and carefully place on the prepared baking sheet. Bake for 10 to 15 minutes, until crisp.

off-the-beaten-path
trail mix

TOTAL TIME 10 min.　|　**ACTIVE TIME** 10 min.　|　**SERVINGS** 8+

Trail mix is a perfect recipe to let children help make. There are endless variations, and it is great added to school lunches or served alone as a snack. This is my family's favorite version.

3 cups unsweetened coconut flakes

2 cups sunflower seeds

2 cups pumpkin seeds

2 cups chopped dried pineapple

1 cup raisins

2 cups dark chocolate chips (optional)

Preheat the oven to 350°F.

Place the coconut flakes, sunflower seeds, and pumpkin seeds on a large baking sheet and bake for 5 minutes, or until barely toasted. Remove from the oven and allow the coconut and seeds to cool completely. Add the pineapple, raisins, and, if using, the chocolate chips to the baking sheet and mix all the ingredients.

Store in an airtight container at room temperature for up to 2 weeks.

bacon-guacamole bites
on sweet potato chips

TOTAL TIME 40 min. | **ACTIVE TIME** 10 min. | **SERVINGS** 4

These were born out of a pregnancy craving and became a favorite appetizer and lunch recipe at our house. They combine all of my favorite foods: bacon, sweet potatoes, and guacamole, for a naturally sweet and savory combination.

¼ cup coconut oil

3 medium sweet potatoes

1 teaspoon salt

1 teaspoon freshly ground black pepper

2 ripe avocados

¾ cup salsa

Zest and juice of 1 organic lime

½ teaspoon garlic powder

½ teaspoon ground cumin

½ teaspoon salt

8 slices cooked bacon

1 cup grated white Cheddar cheese (optional)

Preheat the oven to 425°F.

Heat the oil in a small skillet over medium heat. Slice the sweet potatoes into ¼-inch pieces. Toss with the oil and sprinkle with the salt and pepper. Place in a single layer on a large baking sheet and bake for 30 minutes, or until lightly browned. Remove from the oven and let cool completely.

Halve the avocados, remove the pit, and scoop the flesh into a medium bowl. Add the salsa, lime zest and juice, garlic powder, cumin, and salt and mash until just combined but not smooth. Rough-chop the bacon and stir into the guacamole.

Top each sweet potato chip with a scoop of the guacamole mixture and top with a sprinkling of cheese, if using.

turkey-avocado temaki

TOTAL TIME 10 min. | **ACTIVE TIME** 10 min. | **SERVINGS** 4
(2 rolls each)

Temaki, or sushi hand rolls, are simple to make and a more nutritious alternative to sandwiches. Sheets of nori add flavor and nutrition and are a great way to wrap up favorites like turkey and avocado. This version differs from the usual temaki since it doesn't contain any type of fish, but it is more kid friendly with turkey.

1 ripe avocado

1 cucumber

8 nori sheets

8 slices nitrate-free turkey

8 slices Cheddar cheese (optional)

¼ cup homemade ranch dressing (see page 299) or store-bought (optional)

Halve the avocado, remove the pit, and scoop out the flesh. Place in a small bowl and mash until smooth. Julienne the cucumber into thin pieces and set aside.

Lay each nori sheet flat on a sheet of parchment paper or foil. Spread a layer of avocado on one side of each nori sheet at a slight angle so that you will be able to roll it starting with a corner. Place a slice of turkey on each sheet of nori and add a slice of cheese, if using. Evenly divide the julienned cucumber among all the wraps. Drizzle with ranch dressing, if using.

Begin wrapping the nori at one corner and roll at a slight angle so that in the finished roll, one end is open and the other is a tight point. Wrap in parchment paper or foil if packing for a lunch.

tip: Want to keep it more authentic? Substitute smoked salmon for the turkey in this recipe. You can customize this recipe for almost any kind of wrap by changing up the ingredients.

not-so-plain plantain chips

TOTAL TIME 15 min.　ACTIVE TIME 15 min.　SERVINGS 4

Plantains may look like green bananas, but they don't taste like them! They have a much more starchy texture and aren't sweet like bananas. We often make these as a substitute for chips and crackers and serve them with dips and cheese.

3 green plantains

½ cup coconut oil

1 tablespoon salt

1 teaspoon chili powder (see Note, page 297)

Peel the plantains and slice crosswise with a mandoline or a knife as thinly as possible ($\frac{1}{16}$-inch slices are perfect). Heat the oil in a large frying pan over medium-high heat. Working in batches, fry the plantain chips in a single layer. Cook for 2 minutes per side, or until golden brown and crispy.

Remove from the heat and place the chips on a drying rack or paper-towel-lined plate to drain. Sprinkle with salt and chili powder and serve immediately.

chicken blt club wraps

TOTAL TIME 10 min.   **ACTIVE TIME** 10 min.   **SERVINGS** 4

Club sandwiches and BLTs are classic lunch fare, but for a more refreshing and delicious twist, I like to make a hybrid wrap of the two on lettuce leaves. Great to pack for school lunches and a children and adult favorite at our house.

1 head of Bibb or iceberg lettuce

¼ cup Homemade Mayonnaise (page 320) or store-bought

½ pound cooked chicken breasts or thighs

8 slices cooked bacon

1 ripe avocado

1 medium tomato

Wash and dry the lettuce and carefully separate 8 whole leaves from the head. Place the 4 largest leaves on a large flat surface, and place a smaller leaf inside each of the large ones. This will create 4 thicker, more stable shells. Spread each lettuce shell with the mayonnaise. Thinly slice the chicken and divide evenly among the shells. Place 2 pieces of bacon on each. Halve the avocado, remove the pit, scoop out the flesh, and cut it into 8 slices. Divide these evenly among the lettuce shells.

Thinly slice the tomato and place on top. Carefully roll the lettuce shells to create burrito-shaped rolls. Tightly seal the finished wraps in parchment paper or foil if packing for a school lunch.

tip: To mix things up, add some alfalfa sprouts, shaved cucumber slices, or ranch dressing instead of the mayo.

angel-ed eggs
(avocado deviled eggs)

TOTAL TIME 25 min. | **ACTIVE TIME** 10 min. | **SERVINGS** 4

These angel-ed eggs are a guilt-free pleasure with added healthful fats from avocado and a slight zing from lemon zest and juice. Great for school lunches, parties, or breakfasts.

12 large eggs

1 ripe avocado

½ cup Homemade Mayonnaise (page 320) or store-bought

Zest and juice of 1 organic lemon

½ teaspoon salt

½ teaspoon freshly ground black pepper

4 slices cooked bacon

Bring a large pot of water to a boil and carefully add the eggs. Reduce the heat to medium-high and boil for 12 minutes. Drain and add cool water to the pot. When the eggs have completely cooled, carefully peel and slice in half lengthwise. Place the yolks in a food processor.

Halve the avocado, remove the pit, and scoop the flesh into the food processor with the yolks. Add the mayo, lemon zest and juice, salt, and pepper. Pulse in the food processor until smooth.

Spoon or pipe the yolk filling into the egg-white halves. Roughly chop the bacon and sprinkle on top, and serve.

tip: Preboil the eggs on a food-prep day and this recipe comes together in under 10 minutes.

smoked salmon–stuffed celery

TOTAL TIME 10 min.   ACTIVE TIME 10 min.   SERVINGS 8

Ever been asked the question "If you could only eat five foods for the rest of your life, what would they be?" If I had to choose, smoked salmon would be on my list. I love it alone but also love it in simple and refreshing recipes like this one, and this makes a great lunch or snack.

1 head of celery

8 ounces smoked salmon

8 ounces cream cheese, softened

1 teaspoon finely chopped fresh dill

½ teaspoon garlic powder

1 green onion

Trim the dried ends of the celery and discard the leaves. Cut the stalks into 4-inch lengths.

Finely chop the smoked salmon and place in a small bowl. Add the cream cheese, dill, and garlic powder and mix together by hand until evenly combined.

Spoon the salmon and cream cheese mixture into the celery stalks. Very thinly slice the green onion and sprinkle on top. Consume immediately or store in an airtight container in the refrigerator for up to 2 days.

chicken, bacon
& goat cheese—stuffed endive leaves

TOTAL TIME 10 min. | **ACTIVE TIME** 10 min. | **SERVINGS** 6

This recipe has a sophisticated presentation for a party but is simple enough to pack for a school lunch. Chicken, bacon, and goat cheese combine with subtle hints of orange and pecan for a protein-packed fun finger food.

2 heads of Belgium endive

½ pound chicken, cooked and chopped

6 slices bacon, cooked and chopped

12 ounces goat cheese, herbed or garlic flavored, softened

½ cup chopped pecans

Zest and juice of 1 organic orange

Wash and dry the endives. Separate into leaves, place on a cutting board or large platter, and set aside.

Place the chicken and bacon in a medium bowl. Add the goat cheese, pecans, and orange zest and juice and mix by hand until completely combined. Spoon the goat cheese mixture into the endive leaves.

Serve immediately or store in an airtight container in the refrigerator for up to 2 days.

tip: If endive isn't available, spoon the filling into celery boats.

cranberry-pecan chicken salad wraps

TOTAL TIME 10 min. **ACTIVE TIME** 10 min. **SERVINGS** 4

There are endless ways to make chicken salad and I always feel like it is a gamble to order it at restaurants because you can end up with a really good version or a not-so-great one! I prefer to make our own and often make big batches at the beginning of the week to have on hand for lunches throughout the week. Cranberries and honey give this subtle sweetness while celery and pecans give it crunch.

2 pounds cooked skinless, boneless chicken breasts

2 stalks celery

½ cup dried cranberries

½ cup finely chopped pecans

1 cup Homemade Mayonnaise (page 320) or store-bought

1 tablespoon Dijon mustard

½ teaspoon garlic powder

1 teaspoon lemon juice

2 tablespoons honey

1 head of Bibb or iceberg lettuce

Chop the chicken breasts into ¼- to ½-inch cubes and place in a medium bowl. Finely dice the celery and dried cranberries and add to the bowl. Add the pecans, mayo, and mustard. Sprinkle in the garlic powder and add the lemon juice and honey. Mix well to incorporate.

Wash and dry the lettuce and separate into 8 leaves. Scoop the chicken salad into the lettuce leaves, wrap up, and serve.

tuna salad baby tomatoes

TOTAL TIME 15 min.　　**ACTIVE TIME** 15 min.　　**SERVINGS** 4

Who says tuna should be served on whole wheat? I love this simple tuna salad served on baby tomatoes instead! The tomatoes add flavor and an extra vegetable and are easy to prepare.

2 6-ounce cans smoked tuna

1 stalk celery

½ cup Homemade Mayonnaise (page 320) or store-bought

¼ cup dill pickle relish or 1 finely chopped dill pickle

1 tablespoon Dijon mustard

36 cherry tomatoes

Drain the tuna and place in a medium bowl. Finely chop the celery and add to the bowl along with the mayo, relish, and mustard and stir to combine. Cut the tops off the tomatoes and use a small spoon to scoop out the seeds. Fill each tomato with a heaping spoonful of tuna salad.

Serve immediately or pack (with an ice pack) for lunches. Store in an airtight container in the refrigerator for up to 2 days.

tip: Not a tomato fan? This tuna salad is great on its own, over salad, or on top of Grain-Free Garlic-Herb Crackers (page 219) instead!

cheesy buffalo chicken dip

TOTAL TIME 10 min. | **ACTIVE TIME** 10 min. | **SERVINGS** 4

Chicken wings were one of my husband's favorite foods in college and I often re-create a healthful version at home. This dip has the flavor of buffalo chicken wings combined with cream cheese and is excellent served with celery, crackers, or on lettuce leaves.

2 cups shredded cooked chicken

1 tablespoon unsalted butter

8 ounces cream cheese, softened

½ cup Frances's Red Hot Sauce (page 323) or store-bought

1 cup grated Cheddar cheese (optional)

Stalks from 1 head of celery

Heat the chicken in a large skillet over medium heat with the butter. Add the cream cheese in chunks and stir until melted. Pour in the hot sauce and stir to combine. Top with the cheese, if using, until just melted, and remove from the heat.

Serve immediately with celery on the side. This dip is also a wonderful accompaniment to Grain-Free Garlic-Herb Crackers (page 219) or Not-So-Plain Plantain Chips (page 226). It's also delicious cooled and wrapped in lettuce leaves.

Store leftover dip for up to 4 days in the fridge and eat cold or reheat before serving.

cottage pie–stuffed sweet potatoes

TOTAL TIME 45 min. | **ACTIVE TIME** 20 min. | **SERVINGS** 4

I love the flavors of shepherd's pie (with lamb) and cottage pie (with beef) but wanted a simpler one-pan version of this filling meal. On a bulk-cooking day I premade the meat mixture for a cottage pie and realized that I didn't have to mash the sweet potatoes for a topping . . . I could top the sweet potatoes with the meat! This recipe was born, and it has been a regular in our rotation ever since.

4 large sweet potatoes

1 pound ground beef

1 onion

2 carrots

½ cup Beef Bone Broth (page 154) or store-bought

1 teaspoon salt

½ teaspoon freshly ground black pepper

1 tablespoon Italian Seasoning (page 298) or store-bought

1 teaspoon garlic powder

½ cup frozen peas

Preheat the oven to 375°F.

Wash the sweet potatoes and prick with a fork. Place on a large baking sheet and bake for 45 to 60 minutes, until fork tender.

While the sweet potatoes are cooking, in a large skillet over medium-high heat, brown the beef, breaking it up as it cooks, for 8 to 10 minutes. Finely dice the onion and grate the carrots and add to the skillet when the meat is almost done. Cook until the carrots are tender and the onion is translucent, about 3 to 4 minutes.

Stir in the salt, pepper, Italian seasoning, and garlic powder. Add the peas and cook until the peas are warmed through, about 3 minutes. Remove from the heat.

Remove the sweet potatoes from the oven. Cut a slit in the top of each sweet potato, mash slightly to make room inside, and fill with the beef mixture before serving.

tip: If you premake the meat mixture, then you'll have a quick meal that reheats in 10 minutes.

goat cheese–stuffed dates with prosciutto

TOTAL TIME 20 min. ⋮ ACTIVE TIME 10 min. ⋮ SERVINGS 4

I once read a study that suggested that consuming dates daily in the last month of pregnancy could shorten labor. I was willing to give it a try but found dates too sweet on their own, and I wanted to combine them with protein. The saltiness of goat cheese and prosciutto provided a great balance and I found that I really enjoy dates prepared this way.

2 green onions

8 ounces goat cheese, at room temperature

16 Medjool dates, pitted

8 large slices prosciutto

Preheat the oven to 400°F.

Thinly slice the green onions and mash them with the goat cheese to combine. Carefully stuff a small amount of the cheese mixture into each date. Cut the prosciutto slices in half and wrap one half tightly around each date. Bake for 10 minutes, or until the prosciutto is crispy. Remove, let cool, then serve.

homemade gyro
lunch meat

TOTAL TIME 18 hr.   ACTIVE TIME 2 hr.   SERVINGS 12+

This recipe re-creates the flavors of gyro meat found in restaurants and street vendors in Europe. I first tried this meat when visiting Germany in college and was excited when a friend shared a recipe for making it at home. I adapted it to get the flavor and texture I wanted, and now this is a recipe I make often, especially since it can be prepared ahead of time.

2 medium onions

4 garlic cloves

2 pounds ground lamb

1 pound ground beef

1 tablespoon dried marjoram

1 tablespoon dried basil

1 teaspoon dried oregano

½ teaspoon dried thyme

1 tablespoon salt

1 teaspoon freshly ground black pepper

Rough-chop the onions and add to a food processor with the garlic. Process until completely smooth. Pour the onion mixture into the middle of a clean but old towel and wrap up tightly. Wring the towel to remove all the moisture. (Note that the smell will likely never come out of the towel, but please do not skip this step as it greatly helps the final texture and taste of the meat.) Remove the onion mixture to a large bowl and wash the food processor for later use. Add the lamb, beef, marjoram, basil, oregano, thyme, salt, and pepper to the bowl and mix by hand until well incorporated. Place the bowl in the refrigerator, covered, for at least 2 hours to let the flavors meld.

Preheat the oven to 325°F.

In small batches, place the meat in the food processor and pulse until smooth, about 30 seconds. Remove and place in a 9 × 13-inch pan, packing down tightly. Bake for 1 hour, or until it reaches an internal temperature of 170°F.

Remove from the oven, pour off any excess fat, let cool, and remove from the baking dish. Place in an airtight container in the refrigerator for at least 2 hours to cool completely.

When cooled, slice into ¼-inch slices using a sharp knife. If you've ever seen gyro meat roasting on a spit in a restaurant, try to imitate the cutting method of slicing long, thin strips. To reheat, place the strips under the broiler in the oven until the ends are crispy, or heat in a large skillet with butter until crispy.

Serve with Tzatziki Sauce (page 325), thinly sliced red onions, and sliced tomatoes on lettuce leaves for a complete meal.

tip: This recipe is very time intensive to make but well worth the wait. It freezes very well, so I often make a double or triple batch and freeze in an airtight container for up to 2 months to have on hand on busy nights.

antipasto kebabs

TOTAL TIME 10 min. | **ACTIVE TIME** 10 min. | **SERVINGS** 12

Kebabs are a staple at my yearly Christmas party and a flavorful lunch idea that can be made in just 10 minutes. My kids enjoy practically any food on a skewer and these are no exception.

1 8-ounce jar green olives

1 8-ounce jar Kalamata olives

1 15-ounce jar roasted red peppers

1 16-ounce jar pepperoncini

1 16-ounce jar marinated artichoke hearts

½ pound dry salami

½ pound mozzarella cheese

12 small bamboo skewers

Drain the olives, red peppers, pepperoncini, and artichoke hearts by opening the lid and carefully pouring out the liquid (using the lid to keep any of the contents from falling out). Slice the dry salami into thin slices. Cut the mozzarella into 1-inch cubes.

On each skewer, thread 1 green olive, 1 red pepper, 1 pepperoncino, 1 artichoke heart, 1 Kalamata olive, 1 folded-over slice of salami, and 1 cube of cheese. Serve immediately or store in an airtight container in the refrigerator for up to 2 days.

caprese blt skewers

TOTAL TIME 10 min. | ACTIVE TIME 10 min. | SERVINGS 6

A flavorful combination of a caprese salad and a BLT on a toothpick skewer makes a great appetizer or addition to a school lunch.

24 cherry or grape tomatoes

12 mozzarella balls

12 toothpicks

1 bunch of fresh basil

12 slices cooked bacon

Halve the tomatoes and mozzarella balls. Place half of a tomato on a toothpick, then a mozzarella half, 1 basil leaf, a folded-over slice of bacon, and finally, another tomato half.

Repeat with the remaining toothpicks.

sweet treats

All you need is love.
But a little chocolate now and then doesn't hurt.

—CHARLES M. SCHULZ

penny's pumpkin pie

TOTAL TIME 1 hr. | ACTIVE TIME 20 min. | MAKES one 9-inch pie

I was never a fan of pumpkin pie until a bumper crop in our garden required me to puree and can or freeze to preserve it and I was searching for pumpkin puree recipes. The most obvious answer was, of course, pumpkin pie, so my kids and I experimented with recipes until we created this one. Not too sweet and not too thick with just the right amount of cinnamon. The kids decided to name it after our cat, Penelope, who jumped on the table and tried it herself!

for the crust

3 tablespoons coconut oil, plus more for greasing

1 cup almond flour

1 egg

½ teaspoon ground cinnamon, or to taste

for the filling

2 cups pureed pumpkin or 1 15-ounce can of store-bought (see Note)

3 eggs

¼ cup raw honey, or to taste

1 tablespoon Pumpkin Pie Spice (page 305)

1 teaspoon vanilla extract

½ cup Coconut Milk (page 278)

Preheat the oven to 325°F. Grease a 9-inch pie pan with the oil and set aside.

To make the crust: In a food processor, finely powder the almond flour and add the egg and cinnamon and pulse until combined and a ball forms. Press the pie dough into the bottom and sides of the prepared pie pan and put in the oven for 10 to 15 minutes, until just beginning to brown.

To make the filling: In the food processor (no need for extra dishes!), combine the pumpkin, eggs, honey, pumpkin pie spice, and vanilla and mix until smooth and spreadable, but not really pourable. Add the coconut milk, a little at a time, until about the consistency of applesauce. You may not need to use all of the coconut milk to achieve this.

Remove the crust from the oven. Pour the filling into the crust and smooth over evenly. Bake for about 1 hour, or until the center is no longer jiggly. It will set more as it cools. Coconut cream or whipped heavy cream along with some chopped pecans make perfect toppings.

note: 15 ounces canned pumpkin puree (nothing added) = approximately 2 cups home-cooked pureed pumpkin with excess liquid drained.

chewy chocolate chip cookies

TOTAL TIME 20 min. | **ACTIVE TIME** 10 min. | **SERVINGS** 4

Chocolate chip cookies are the only dessert my husband really enjoys, and I experimented for months to find a more healthy higher-protein version. I finally stumbled on this version, and it is my go-to cookie recipe these days.

2 cups almond flour

½ cup cane sugar

½ teaspoon baking soda

Pinch of sea salt

½ cup coconut oil or 8 tablespoons (1 stick) unsalted butter, softened

1 large egg

1 tablespoon vanilla extract

1 cup dark chocolate chips, or to taste

Preheat the oven to 350°F.

In a large bowl, mix the flour, sugar, baking soda, and salt. Add the oil and stir until mixed. A thick dough will form. Add the egg and vanilla and mix well. If the dough is too thick and hard to mix, add 1 or 2 teaspoons milk or water to thin. Add the chocolate chips and stir by hand until incorporated.

Form the dough into tablespoon-size balls and bake on a silicone mat or a greased baking sheet for 10 minutes, or until the tops are golden brown. Remove from the oven. The centers will still be somewhat soft, but they will continue to harden while cooling. Let cool at least 5 minutes and serve.

perfect pecan pie

TOTAL TIME 50 min.   **ACTIVE TIME** 20 min.   **SERVINGS** 4

I'm from the South and pecan pie is a common dessert that is served at most holidays and gatherings. While the taste is wonderful, I'm not a fan of the corn syrup and refined sweeteners that most recipes call for, so I created this more nutritious version without the refined sugars for our family get-togethers.

for the crust

2 cups almond flour

1 tablespoon coconut flour (optional)

1 teaspoon gelatin powder

½ cup coconut oil, solid, or 8 tablespoons (1 stick) cold unsalted butter

2 teaspoons coconut sugar

1 egg yolk

for the filling

1 cup pure maple syrup

3 tablespoons coconut oil or butter

½ cup coconut sugar

1 teaspoon vanilla

3 large eggs

1½ cups pecans

Preheat oven to 375°F.

To make the crust: Place the almond flour, coconut flour, if using, and gelatin powder in a food processor and pulse until powdered and combined. Add the oil, the sugar, and the egg yolk and pulse until it forms a ball. Press the dough into an ungreased 9-inch pie pan (or 8 × 8-inch baking dish) and set aside.

To make the filling: In a small saucepan over high heat, simmer the maple syrup for about 5 minutes, or until it reaches a temperature of 225°F and starts to bubble up. (Watch it carefully, as it will overflow quickly once it starts to bubble.)

Pour the syrup into a large bowl and add the oil, sugar, and vanilla. Use an immersion blender to combine, then add the eggs and blend until smooth.

Pour the filling over the pie crust and arrange the top with the pecans. Bake for 30 minutes, or until the center is mostly set. Do not overbake!

Let the pie cool completely before serving. Store at room temperature for up to 24 hours or in the refrigerator for up to 4 days.

matcha key lime pie

| TOTAL TIME 25 min. | ACTIVE TIME 15 min. | MAKES one 9-inch pie |

I fell in love with handmade key lime pie at a family-owned restaurant on my honeymoon and was forever ruined for the premade version. I was able to re-create the recipe after much experimentation but could never get the color green enough until I thought of adding matcha tea!

¼ cup almond flour

¼ cup coconut flour

¼ cup coconut sugar

1 egg

1 teaspoon vanilla extract

4 tablespoons (½ stick) unsalted butter, melted

2 cups sweetened condensed milk (see Note)

Zest and juice of 8 organic limes

4 egg yolks

1 teaspoon matcha green tea powder

Preheat the oven to 350°F.

Place the almond and coconut flours, sugar, egg, vanilla, and butter in a food processor and pulse until mixed. If needed, add a little bit of water to make moist enough to form a ball of dough. Press the dough into a 9-inch pie pan.

In a small bowl, whisk together the sweetened condensed milk, lime zest and juice, egg yolks, and matcha powder and pour into the prepared crust.

Bake for about 15 minutes, or until starting to set but not solid. Remove and let cool. Cover and refrigerate overnight before serving.

note: To make enough homemade sweetened condensed milk for this recipe, simmer 3 cups whole milk in a medium saucepan. Add 1 cup unrefined sugar and simmer on very low heat for 3 hours, until reduced by half. Let cool and use.

protein-packed chocolate mousse

TOTAL TIME 20 min. | **ACTIVE TIME** 10 min. | **SERVINGS** 6

A tribute to my mom's French heritage. This delicious and simple chocolate mousse combines eggs and dark chocolate for a protein-packed treat that both kids and adults love.

8 tablespoons (1 stick) unsalted butter

1 teaspoon honey or maple syrup

10 ounces dark chocolate chips

8 large eggs, separated

¼ teaspoon salt

Melt the butter, honey, and chocolate in a double boiler until just melted. Remove from the heat and let cool slightly.

Separate the eggs. Put the egg whites in a large mixing bowl and set aside. Add the egg yolks one at a time to the melted chocolate mixture and whisk quickly to combine.

Add the salt to the egg whites and beat with a hand mixer or whisk them vigorously until stiff peaks form, about 5 minutes. (The salt helps achieve stiff peaks faster.)

Very gently, add the chocolate mixture to the egg whites and combine with a spatula.

Refrigerate overnight in this bowl or transfer to the dish you plan to serve in before refrigerating.

tip: For a fancier presentation when serving, transfer the mousse to small dessert cups or jars before refrigerating and shave pieces of chocolate over the top before serving. It can also be spooned into a piping or pastry bag after refrigerating and squeezed into the container of choice to serve.

dairy-free panna cotta

TOTAL TIME 6 hr.   **ACTIVE TIME** 15 min.   **SERVINGS** 4

This delicious dessert uses almond and coconut milks for a light and mildly sweet dessert. My little kids say that these "taste like clouds," and all of my kids enjoy helping make this recipe.

2 cups Coconut Milk (page 278) or unsweetened full-fat store-bought

2 cups Almond Milk (page 278) or unsweetened store-bought

2 tablespoons plus 1 teaspoon unflavored gelatin

3 tablespoons raw honey

3 tablespoons maple syrup

2 teaspoons vanilla extract

1 teaspoon coconut oil

Pour the coconut and almond milks into a medium saucepan and gently whisk in the gelatin. Wait 5 minutes to allow the gelatin to soften, then place the saucepan on medium heat. Add the honey, maple syrup, and vanilla, stirring constantly, until the milk is hot enough to steam. Do not boil as this will deactivate the gelling properties of the gelatin.

Lightly grease four small bowls or molds with the coconut oil and pour the heated mixture evenly among them. Cover and place in the refrigerator until set, at least 5 hours. Serve as is or gently turn them upside down onto a plate and add toppings like fresh strawberries or slivers of dark chocolate.

simple chia seed pudding

TOTAL TIME 12 hr. **ACTIVE TIME** 4 min. **SERVINGS** 4

Chia seeds are nutrient powerhouses and this pudding is so delicious that it is hard to believe it is so good for you! I premake this throughout the week to have on hand for breakfasts or as a nourishing dessert.

2 cups Coconut Milk (page 278) or full-fat store-bought

½ teaspoon vanilla extract

¼ cup maple syrup, or to taste

¼ teaspoon ground cinnamon (optional)

½ cup chia seeds

For a blended/smooth version: Place all the ingredients in a blender and blend on high for 1 to 2 minutes, until completely smooth.

For a whole chia seed version (my favorite): Place the coconut milk, vanilla, maple syrup, and cinnamon, if using, in a blender on high for 1 to 2 minutes, until smooth. Whisk in the chia seeds until combined.

For both: Pour the mixture into a jar or glass container and place in the refrigerator, covered, for at least 4 hours to let gel. I prefer to make this at night to have ready for a fast breakfast the next day. It is also great to make in the morning for a delicious premade dessert at night.

chocolate-cherry bark
with coconut oil

TOTAL TIME 15 min. | **ACTIVE TIME** 15 min. | **SERVINGS** 4

Inspired by my dad and his love of chocolate-covered cherries at Christmas, this coconut oil–based chocolate bark has sweetness from dried cherries and crunch from pecans and coconut flakes. A nutritious treat packed with beneficial fats and lots of flavor!

1 cup pecans, chopped

¼ cup unsweetened coconut flakes

1 cup unrefined coconut oil (must be unrefined so it is solid at room temperature)

¾ cup cocoa powder

¾ cup maple syrup, or to taste

½ cup dried cherries

Preheat the oven to 325°F. Prepare a baking sheet lined with parchment paper and set aside.

Place the pecans and coconut flakes on a large baking sheet, spreading into a single layer.

Toast in the oven for 6 to 8 minutes, until toasted, but watch closely, as the coconut will toast very quickly. Remove from the oven and let cool.

Heat the oil in a medium saucepan over medium heat. Remove from the heat. Whisk in the cocoa powder and maple syrup. Taste and add more syrup if desired.

Spread the cocoa mixture evenly onto the prepared baking sheet; it should be less than ½ inch thick. While still warm, sprinkle with the toasted nuts and dried cherries and press them in lightly. Place in the freezer on the baking sheet for 15 to 20 minutes, until hardened. Remove and cut or break into pieces. Store in an airtight container in the freezer until ready to eat. This will store for up to 1 month in the freezer.

tip: Don't want to make your own chocolate? Use 1 pound premade dark chocolate, melt in a double boiler, and pour onto a lined baking sheet. Add toppings and freeze. This will also create a more firm chocolate for packing for lunches if needed.

baked cinnamon-chia apples

TOTAL TIME 55 min. **ACTIVE TIME** 10 min. **SERVINGS** 6

When I was growing up, fruit was often served for dessert or used in warm dessert recipes. These delicious and simple baked apples are a flashback to my childhood, but I've updated them with the warm flavor of cinnamon and protein from pecans and chia seeds.

6 large apples, such as Honeycrisp or Golden Delicious

1 cup pecans

½ cup chia seeds

¼ cup coconut oil or 4 tablespoons (½ stick) unsalted butter

3 tablespoons ground cinnamon

½ cup coconut sugar, or more to taste

Preheat the oven to 375°F.

Use a sharp knife or melon baller to scoop out the core of each apple, starting at the top and leaving about ½ inch at the bottom to hold the filling. Place the apples in a greased medium baking dish and set aside.

In a food processor, pulse the pecans and chia seeds for 3 to 4 seconds, until combined and finely chopped, but not powdered. Add the oil, cinnamon, and sugar and pulse once to combine.

Carefully spoon the cinnamon and nut mixture into the middle of the cored apples, packing extra filling on top. Add ½ inch of water to the baking dish, being careful not to get any liquid inside the apples. Bake for 45 minutes, or until the apples are tender and the filling is browned and fragrant, checking once to make sure there is water remaining in the pan. Serve warm or store in the refrigerator for up to 3 days and reheat before serving.

slow cooker apple butter

TOTAL TIME 12 hr. 10 min. | **ACTIVE TIME** 10 min. | **SERVINGS** 12

I first discovered apple butter when I read *Little House on the Prairie* as a child, and I asked my mom if we could try making it. I've been making, and tweaking, this recipe ever since, and now I enjoy this all-day apple butter with my kids!

10 pounds apples

¼ cup apple cider vinegar

½ cup apple cider

2 tablespoons ground cinnamon

½ teaspoon nutmeg

½ teaspoon ground cloves

½ cup coconut sugar, or more to taste (optional)

Peel, core, and slice the apples and place in a 6-quart slow cooker. Add the vinegar and cider. Cook on low for 8 to 10 hours (overnight works really well), until completely soft.

Blend with an immersion blender until completely smooth. Stir in the cinnamon, nutmeg, cloves, and, if using, the sugar. (This recipe doesn't really need any sugar, as apples are naturally sweet and the sweetness intensifies with a long cooking time, but some people prefer the added sweetness.)

Leave the slow cooker uncovered and cook for another 1 to 2 hours on low to let thicken to the desired thickness. Store in airtight jars in the refrigerator for up to 3 weeks or the freezer for up to 1 year.

tip: Make this recipe before going to bed and enjoy for breakfast in the morning.

no-bake meyer lemon bars

TOTAL TIME 25 min. | **ACTIVE TIME** 15 min. | **SERVINGS** 6

A simple lemon curd recipe with an almond flour crust, these lemon bars are great as a dessert after a fancy dinner or as an addition to a school lunch!

1½ cups almond flour

1 tablespoon gelatin powder

1 cup coconut oil or ghee, or 8 tablespoons (1 stick) unsalted butter

2 tablespoons coconut sugar, or to taste

1 teaspoon vanilla extract

3 organic Meyer lemons (see Note)

2 eggs

3 egg yolks

¼ cup honey or maple syrup

In a food processor, pulse the flour, gelatin, ½ cup oil, sugar, and vanilla until it forms a ball. Taste for sweetness and add more sugar if desired. Press the mixture into an 8 × 8-inch baking dish and set aside.

Zest and juice the lemons into a glass measuring cup and set aside.

Place the eggs and egg yolks in a small saucepan over low heat. Add the honey, lemon zest and juice, and the remaining ½ cup oil. Blend with an immersion blender until well combined, then raise the heat to medium-low and cook for an additional 5 to 10 minutes, pulsing constantly with the immersion blender until the mixture thickens and the sides start to bubble.

Ladle the mixture through a fine-mesh strainer (optional but recommended), using a spoon to help push the mixture through the strainer if needed. Pour over the crust and refrigerate immediately. Allow to set in the refrigerator for at least 3 hours before serving.

note: Meyer lemons are the best in this recipe, but any lemons will work and even limes or blood oranges make a great substitute in a pinch!

chocolate-avocado
ice cream

| TOTAL TIME 3 hr. 15 min. | ACTIVE TIME 15 min. | SERVINGS 8 |

Creamy dairy-free ice cream with a nutrient-rich avocado and coconut milk base, magnesium-rich cocoa powder, and just a hint of natural sweetener. Let the kids help you make this delicious and simple dessert!

3 very ripe avocados

2 cups Coconut Milk (page 278) or heavy cream

½ cup unsweetened cocoa powder

¾ cup maple syrup, or to taste

1 tablespoon vanilla extract

Halve the avocados, remove the pits, and scoop the flesh into a blender. Add the coconut milk, cocoa powder, maple syrup, and vanilla and blend on high until smooth. Taste and correct for the desired sweetness, adding more cocoa powder or maple syrup if needed. Place the blender in the refrigerator for at least 3 hours to cool completely. Pour the mixture into an ice cream maker and follow the manufacturer's directions. This recipe will set quickly!

Serve immediately or store in an airtight container in the freezer for up to 1 month until ready to consume. Let it defrost slightly for 3 to 4 minutes before serving for the best texture.

tip: Don't have an ice cream maker? Have some kids? Turn this into a science lesson: Put 2 cups at a time of the ice cream mixture into a quart-size plastic or silicone food bag. Place the bag inside a larger bag or a coffee can. Add ice and ¼ cup salt to the outer bag, making sure not to get any inside the bag with the ice cream mixture. Let your kids shake or roll the bag or can for 5 to 10 minutes, until the ice cream in the inner bag sets to the desired firmness. Remove, carefully rinse the inner bag to remove any clinging salt, and serve!

delightful drinks

I cook with wine, sometimes I even add it to the food.

—W. C. FIELDS

supercharged hot cocoa recipe

TOTAL TIME 5 min. | **ACTIVE TIME** 5 min. | **SERVINGS** 1

Make this incredibly simple hot chocolate with gelatin for added protein, and upgrade your hot chocolate with the addition of cinnamon, turmeric, and even a pinch of cayenne for better absorption and taste!

8 ounces hot water or Coconut Milk (page 278), about 180°F

2 tablespoons cocoa powder

1 tablespoon gelatin powder

1 tablespoon coconut oil

1 pinch ground cayenne pepper (optional)

½ teaspoon ground turmeric (optional)

½ teaspoon ground cinnamon (optional)

1 teaspoon maple syrup, honey, or stevia drops, or to taste (optional)

½ teaspoon vanilla extract (optional)

Place the water, cocoa powder, gelatin powder, oil, and, if using, the cayenne, turmeric, cinnamon, maple syrup, and vanilla in a blender and blend on high until smooth. Serve warm and enjoy!

supermom coffee varieties

As a mom, coffee is one of my best friends, and not for the caffeine. In fact, I often drink decaf coffee, herbal coffee, or chai tea in place of regular coffee, but I supercharge my coffee with some nutrient-dense add-ins to give myself extra energy. As a bonus, these additional ingredients are great for hair, skin, and nails, so my morning indulgence is part of my beauty routine, too! Not a mom? Don't let the name fool you. This coffee is great for dads and kids, too!

basic supermom coffee

1 cup brewed coffee, herbal coffee, or tea of choice

1 teaspoon coconut oil

1 teaspoon butter

1 teaspoon collagen powder

½ of a vanilla bean (scrape out the seeds with the back of a knife and discard the pod) or ½ teaspoon vanilla extract

½ teaspoon pure maple syrup

Put all the ingredients in a blender. Blend on high speed for 20 seconds, until frothy. Drink immediately and enjoy all the energy!

spiced pumpkin latte supermom coffee

To Basic Supermom Coffee, add ½ teaspoon Pumpkin Pie Spice (page 305) and 1 tablespoon pumpkin puree.

peppermint mocha supermom coffee

To Basic Supermom Coffee, add 1 tablespoon cocoa powder and a few drops of peppermint-flavored stevia extract or peppermint extract to taste.

salted caramel latte supermom coffee

Omit the maple syrup from Basic Supermom Coffee and add 1 teaspoon raw honey and a pinch of Himalayan or other sea salt.

gingerbread latte recipe

Omit the maple syrup from Basic Supermom Coffee and instead add 1 teaspoon blackstrap molasses and ¼ teaspoon ground cinnamon powder.

herbal coffee

Not a fan of coffee? Use this herbal recipe as the base for supermom coffee instead!

1 teaspoon dandelion root

1 teaspoon roasted chicory root (optional)

1 teaspoon roasted carob pods

1 teaspoon maca powder

Pour 1 cup boiling water over the dandelion, chicory, and carob pods in a coffee mug and let brew for 5 to 8 minutes. Strain out the herbs and add the liquid to a blender. Blend with the maca powder until frothy and use as the base for these coffee recipes.

homemade dairy-free "milk" recipes

When we found out that our son had a dairy allergy, I had to find alternatives to dairy milk to use in recipes. Most store-bought dairy-free milks were expensive and had additives I wanted to avoid, so I started making my own and we still use these recipes to save time and money!

coconut milk

1½ to 2 cups unsweetened shredded coconut

4 cups water

Heat the water to about 180°F but do not boil.

Put the coconut in a blender and add the water. (If your blender is not large enough to accommodate this entire recipe, use half of the water and half of the coconut and make in two batches.) Blend on high speed for 3 minutes, until thick and creamy. Ladle the mixture through a fine-mesh sieve to get most of the coconut out and then squeeze through a clean towel or several thicknesses of cheesecloth to remove any remaining pieces of coconut. Drink immediately or store in the refrigerator for up to 4 days. Since there are no preservatives or fillers, the "cream" of the coconut milk may separate on the top after storing. Just shake or stir before using.

tip: Flavor options: After all the coconut has been strained out, try adding the following: ½ teaspoon vanilla extract, ½ cup fresh or frozen strawberries, or 2 teaspoons cocoa powder + ½ teaspoon vanilla to the entire batch and blend on high until smooth and incorporated.

almond milk

1 cup raw almonds

4 cups filtered water

1 vanilla bean (optional)

4 pitted dates (optional)

1 teaspoon honey or 4 drops liquid stevia (optional)

Soak the almonds in the water for at least 12 hours, until sprouted. Rinse well and place in a blender. Blend on high speed for 3 to 5 minutes, until smooth and creamy. Warning: The mixture will expand by about ⅓ (depending on your blender), so make sure your blender is not full before starting it; you may need to work in batches. Ladle the mixture into a large bowl through a sprout bag, cheesecloth, or kitchen towel and squeeze to remove all the liquid. Return the milk back to the blender, and, if using, add the seeds of the vanilla bean, soaked dates, or honey. Pour into a glass jar or pitcher and store in the refrigerator for up to 1 week.

tip: Save the pulp of the almonds, put on a cookie sheet, and dehydrate in the oven on the lowest heat until completely dry. Run through a blender or food processor to make the almond flour, which can be used in recipes in place of flour.

cashew milk

1 cup raw cashews

8 cups filtered water

½ teaspoon sea salt

1 vanilla bean or 1 teaspoon vanilla extract (optional)

Dates, honey, or stevia (optional)

Soak the cashews for at least 12 hours in 4 cups of the filtered water with the salt. Rinse well and place the remaining filtered water and the cashews in a blender. Blend on high speed for 3 to 5 minutes, until smooth and creamy. Warning: The mixture will expand by about ⅓ (depending on your blender), so make sure your blender is not full before starting it; you may need to work in batches.

Ladle the mixture into a large bowl through a sprout bag, cheesecloth, or kitchen towel and squeeze to remove all the liquid. Return the milk back to the blender, and, if using, add the seeds of the vanilla bean, the soaked dates, or the honey. Blend it on high speed until it is completely smooth. Pour into a glass jar or pitcher and store in the refrigerator for up to 1 week.

herbal teas and blends
single herb teas and infusions

chamomile calmer tea

Chamomile flower tea is one of the most consumed teas in the world behind regular black tea. The flowers have a naturally sweet taste with a hint of an apple flavor. Chamomile is a good herbal source of magnesium and is known as a soothing and relaxing herb.

To brew, use 1 tablespoon dried chamomile flowers per 1 cup water. Pour the boiling water over the herbs, cover to keep in the beneficial oils, and let steep for at least 5 minutes. Strain out the herbs using a fine-mesh strainer and drink immediately.

simple mint tea

Mint tea is probably second to chamomile in popularity among herbal teas. Peppermint tea soothes the digestive tract and is helpful for heartburn, nausea, and indigestion. While it is especially helpful during illness, peppermint is a delicious tea anytime and can be consumed alone or with other herbs to help increase their effectiveness.

To brew, use 1 tablespoon dried peppermint leaf per 1 cup water. Pour the boiling water over the herbs, cover to keep in the beneficial oils, and let steep for at least 5 minutes. Strain out the herbs using a fine-mesh strainer and drink immediately.

raspberry leaf infusion

Raspberry leaf is often consumed during pregnancy, as it is a good source of magnesium, potassium, and B vitamins. It has a taste similar to regular black tea and can be combined with stevia leaf to make a naturally sweet tea. I drink it hot in the winter and cold during the summer months; my kids like it iced (and sometimes with chia seeds in it).

To brew hot tea by the cup, use 1 tablespoon dried raspberry leaf per 1 cup water. Pour the boiling water over the herbs, cover with a lid to keep in the beneficial oils, and let steep for at least 5 minutes. Strain out the herbs using a fine-mesh strainer and drink immediately.

To brew by the gallon and drink cold: Add ¾ cup of loose dried raspberry leaf to 1 gallon boiling water. Remove from the heat, cover, and let steep for at least 30 minutes (it may be steeped for up to 8 hours). Strain out the herbs, add 1 tablespoon honey or other sweetener if desired, and store in the refrigerator for 2 to 5 days.

alfalfa vitamin tea

A powerhouse of nutrients and a great dietary source of many vitamins as well as chlorophyll, which is said to help digestion and help reduce body odor, alfalfa is often added to other herbs in teas but is excellent on its own, too.

To brew, use 1 tablespoon dried alfalfa leaf per 1 cup water. Pour the boiling water over the alfalfa and let steep for at least 10 minutes. Add honey or the sweetener of choice if desired.

dandelion detox tea

Dandelion is said to nourish organs like the liver, kidneys, and gallbladder and is often given to promote liver health. The entire dandelion plant can be used (root, flower, and leaves/stem), though the leaves are the most gentle tasting and the best for a soothing tea.

To brew, use 1 tablespoon dried dandelion leaf per 8 ounces of water. Pour the boiling water over the herbs, cover to keep in the beneficial oils, and let steep for at least 5 minutes.

hibiscus vitamin c tea

Hibiscus is a bright red flower with a bitter taste and a high concentration of vitamin C. It is often used in herbal blends or for its color in natural cosmetics. For a natural vitamin C infusion, hibiscus tea can be used alone.

To brew, use 1 tablespoon dried hibiscus per 1 cup water. Pour the boiling water over the herbs, cover to keep in the beneficial oils, and let steep for at least 5 minutes. Since hibiscus is so bitter, I suggest sweetening with 1 teaspoon dried stevia leaf or 4 drops liquid stevia tincture or 1 teaspoon raw honey.

ginger digestive tea

Ginger is the master herb for digestion and also helps soothe nausea and upset stomach. It is best used fresh, as the dried spice loses some of its potency.

To brew, mince a 1-inch piece of peeled fresh ginger per 1 cup water. Pour the boiling water over it, cover to keep in the beneficial oils, and let steep for at least 5 minutes.

herbal tea blends

sleep easy blend

My go-to tea when I am having trouble sleeping is an equal mixture of chamomile, peppermint, and catnip herbs.

To brew, use 1 teaspoon each of dried chamomile, mint, and catnip leaves per 1 cup water. Pour the boiling water over the herbs, cover to keep in the beneficial oils, and let steep for at least 5 minutes.

lavender tea

Lavender is my favorite scent and essential oil, but it is too strong to be used alone in a tea. This is my favorite lavender tea recipe.

½ **cup dried mint leaf**

2 tablespoons dried lavender

2 tablespoons stevia (optional)

In a small bowl, mix together all the ingredients and store in a cool, dark place in an airtight container. Use 1 to 2 teaspoons dried herbal mix per 1 cup water to make hot or iced tea.

chai tea

Chai tea is a favorite around our house, and we usually make it with raspberry leaf tea instead of black tea and with coconut milk instead of regular milk.

½ cup loose-leaf black tea or herbal tea or 8 tea bags (I use raspberry leaf)

1 to 2 teaspoons stevia leaf

8 thin slices of fresh peeled ginger or ½ teaspoon ground ginger (optional)

6 cinnamon sticks

8 to 10 whole cloves or ¼ to ½ teaspoon ground cloves

2 cardamom pods (optional but really good)

1 tablespoon chamomile flowers (optional)

½ teaspoon dried fennel seeds (optional)

4 cups Coconut Milk (page 278) or store-bought

1 teaspoon vanilla extract

Put 4 cups of water in a 6-quart slow cooker. Place the black tea, stevia leaf, ginger, cinnamon, cloves, and, if using, the cardamom, chamomile, and fennel in a cloth bag and add to the slow cooker. Cook on high for 2 to 2½ hours, or on low for up to 6 hours (I've kept it on low overnight), until well steeped and fragrant. Add the coconut milk and vanilla and stir until heated. Serve plain or topped with the cream from a can of coconut milk. This tea can also be chilled and blended with ice and 2 tablespoons coconut oil for an iced version!

stomach soother tea

To ease stomachaches or other digestive troubles, this tea is very soothing.

2 teaspoons dried mint leaf

½ teaspoon dried fennel seeds

Pinch of ground ginger (optional)

Place the mint, fennel seeds, and ginger, if using, in a cup. Pour in 1 cup boiling water, cover to keep in the beneficial oils, and let steep for at least 5 minutes. For a longer-lasting soothing effect, you can also add 1 tablespoon unflavored gelatin powder.

ginger-molasses switchel

TOTAL TIME 5 min.	ACTIVE TIME 5 min.	SERVINGS 4

Switchel is another recipe I remember from my days of reading *Little House on the Prairie* as a child. It combines apple cider vinegar (which contains B vitamins) with molasses (which contains iron and magnesium) to create a hydrating and refreshing drink.

2 tablespoons apple cider vinegar, containing "the mother"

3 tablespoons blackstrap molasses, or more to taste

2 tablespoons finely minced peeled fresh ginger

4 cups filtered water, or 2 cups filtered water and 2 cups seltzer water

Zest and juice of ½ organic lime

Mix all the ingredients in a large jar, shake well, and place in the refrigerator overnight. Strain it through a fine-mesh strainer and store up to 4 days in the refrigerator. Serve over ice.

probiotic lemonade

TOTAL TIME 24 hr. | **ACTIVE TIME** 15 min. | **SERVINGS** 4

A simple homemade lemonade with an added twist: probiotics! Adding whey and fermenting creates a tangy and naturally probiotic-rich drink that kids and adults both love.

2 cups full-fat plain yogurt

1 cup cane sugar

1 sterile gallon-size glass jar

Filtered water

Juice of 12 lemons (about 1 cup)

2 drops stevia (optional)

Wrap the yogurt in a cheesecloth or a clean kitchen towel and hang above a bowl for a few hours to let the liquid drip out. The liquid is the whey and you should end up with about ½ cup for this recipe. Set this aside and reserve the yogurt for another use.

Pour the sugar into the glass jar and add just enough hot water to dissolve the sugar. Add the lemon juice and fill the jar about three-quarters full with filtered water. Make sure the liquid is at room temperature (the hot water may have warmed it), then add the whey.

Cover tightly with a clean towel or a coffee filter and a rubber band to secure, and let sit on the counter out of direct sunlight for 2 to 3 days. The longer it sits, the less sugar in the final product. Place in the refrigerator, where the flavor will continue to develop. Since the sugar diminishes during fermentation, this lemonade can prove rather tart. If it's too tart, you can add the stevia. Enjoy 4 to 6 ounces a day. Store in the refrigerator for 4 days.

kombucha fermented tea varieties

Kombucha is a lightly sweetened fermented tea that has been around for centuries. This refreshing drink can be double-fermented to create a natural carbonation. Health benefits attributed to kombucha include improved digestion, increased energy, and skin improvements.

1 gallon filtered water

1 cup granulated sugar, preferably organic

1 family-size tea bag or 8 to 10 small tea bags

1 sterile gallon-size glass jar

½ cup unflavored store-bought kombucha, such as G.T.s

1 SCOBY (see Note, page 288)

Coffee filter or cheesecloth and a rubber band

4 quart-size glass mason jars

Bring the water and sugar to a boil in a large pot. Add the tea bag and remove from the heat. Let the tea cool to room temperature! This is very important, since tea that is too warm can kill your SCOBY.

Pour the cooled tea into the glass jar, leaving just over 1 inch of room at the top. Pour in the kombucha, and with very clean hands, gently place the SCOBY at the top of the jar of tea. It should float, though if it doesn't, just let it fall and don't stick your hands in the tea! Cover the jar with the coffee filter and secure tightly with the rubber band (fruit flies love this stuff!). Put the jar in a warm (70°F to 75°F degrees is best) corner of the kitchen where it is at least a few feet away from any other fermenting products and out of direct sunlight.

Let the tea ferment, undisturbed, for about 7 days, though the length of time may vary depending on ambient temperature. You can test the kombucha by placing a straw in the jar carefully (slide under the SCOBY) and sipping. It should taste tart but still very slightly sweet also. After the first couple of batches, a "baby" SCOBY will form on top of the original and this is an indication that the kombucha is done as well, but it may not form with the first batch.

At this point, the kombucha is ready for a second fermentation, which will add carbonation but is otherwise optional. If you aren't doing the second fermentation, just pour the kombucha into the quart-size mason jars with airtight lids and keep tightly sealed at room temperature until ready to drink. If you do choose to do the second fermentation, see Tip.

note: SCOBY stands for "symbiotic culture of bacteria and yeast." It is sometimes called "the mother." Dehydrated SCOBY can be purchased from wellnessmama .com/go/kombucha/. Once you begin making kombucha, your tea will naturally produce a new SCOBY, called "the daughter," which you can use to make future batches. If you end up with extra SCOBYs, you can pass them on to friends (along with 1 cup of brewed kombucha in a jar) so they can make kombucha, or compost them.

tip: If you want to create a kombucha "soda" with natural carbonation through a second ferment, you will also need:

1 sterile gallon-size jar or 5 quart-size jars

About 1 quart of fruit juice (we prefer grape or apple for this) or ½ cup frozen berries

Fill the jar three-quarters of the way with the cooled kombucha (without the SCOBY). Fill the rest of the jar with the juice or fruit and cover with an airtight lid. Leave out for 1 or 2 more days at room temperature, checking every 8 hours or so to make sure that the pressure has not built up too much, by opening the jar and listening for a fizz or release of air. Taste-test and when the desired level of carbonation is reached, transfer to the refrigerator to stop fermentation.

kombucha flavor variations

For 1 gallon of kombucha, add:

- 2 cups grape juice

- 2 cups sliced fresh strawberries (or equivalent in frozen strawberries)

- 1 2-inch piece fresh peeled ginger plus 2 cups apple juice

- 1 fresh mango, sliced (strain before using)

- 1 vanilla bean, seeds and pod, split open

- Dried prunes or other fruit

- 1 cup apple juice plus 10 frozen strawberries

- Juice of ½ ruby grapefruit plus 1 teaspoon raw sugar

- ½ cup dried elderberries

- 2 cups apple juice plus 1 cinnamon stick

note: Avoid adding pineapple to kombucha, as it creates a stringy and unappealing final product.

blueberry-ginger shrub

TOTAL TIME 10 min. | **ACTIVE TIME** 10 min. | **SERVINGS** 12

A refreshing fruit, ginger, and tangy vinegar syrup that makes an easy and invigorating addition to a glass of water or club soda for a healthful alternative to soda!

1 cup fresh blueberries

1 cup unrefined sugar

¼ cup minced peeled fresh ginger

1 cup apple cider vinegar

Place the blueberries in a medium glass container with a tight-fitting lid. Add the sugar and ginger and mash to combine. Cover and refrigerate for 2 days. When ready to use, strain through a fine-mesh nonmetal strainer to remove the fruit, and add the vinegar to the remaining liquid. Add the vinegar slowly to get the desired level of tartness. You may not need the entire cup. Add 2 tablespoons to ¼ cup to 1 cup water or club soda for a refreshing and sophisticated drink. Store the shrub syrup in the refrigerator for up to 7 days.

pomegranate-basil shrub

TOTAL TIME 10 min. | **ACTIVE TIME** 10 min. | **SERVINGS** 12

A shrub is a tangy fruit-infused vinegar drink that can be made with fresh fruit or juice. I use pomegranate juice and fresh basil leaves for a refreshing combination in this simple recipe.

1 cup fresh pomegranate juice or store-bought

1 cup apple cider vinegar

1 cup raw honey

½ cup fresh basil leaves

Combine the pomegranate juice, vinegar, and honey in a quart-size glass jar. Muddle or rough-chop the basil leaves and add to the jar and stir. Cover with a lid and let sit for 2 to 3 days in the refrigerator to let the flavors meld.

When ready to use, strain out the basil and store the shrub for up to 3 months in the refrigerator. To serve, add ¼ cup to 1 cup water or club soda for a refreshing nonalcoholic drink.

sauces, seasonings & spices

You learn to cook so that you don't have to be a slave to recipes.
You get what's in season and you know what to do with it.

—JULIA CHILD

curry powder

TOTAL TIME 5 min ⋮ **ACTIVE TIME** 5 min ⋮ **MAKES** 1½ cups

½ cup paprika (see Note, page 297)

¼ cup ground cumin

¼ cup ground turmeric

3 tablespoons ground coriander (optional)

2 tablespoons dry mustard

2 tablespoons ground fenugreek (optional)

1 tablespoon ground fennel

1 tablespoon red pepper flakes (optional)

1 tablespoon ground cardamom (optional)

1 teaspoon ground cinnamon

½ teaspoon ground cloves (optional)

Place the paprika, cumin, turmeric, coriander, if using, dry mustard, fenugreek, if using, fennel, red pepper flakes, if using, cardamom, if using, cinnamon, and cloves, if using, in a 16-ounce or larger airtight jar with a lid and shake well to mix. Store in the jar in the pantry for up to 6 months (or freeze for up to 2 years). Sprinkle on meats, chicken, shrimp, and vegetables and add to soups.

taco seasoning

TOTAL TIME 5 min.　　ACTIVE TIME 5 min.　　MAKES 1 cup

¼ cup chili powder (see Note)

¼ cup ground cumin

¼ cup Himalayan or other sea salt (optional)

1 tablespoon garlic powder

1 tablespoon onion powder (see Note)

1 teaspoon dried oregano

1 teaspoon paprika (see Note)

1 teaspoon freshly ground black pepper

Place the chili powder, cumin, salt, if using, garlic powder, onion powder, oregano, paprika, and pepper in an 8-ounce or larger airtight jar with a lid and shake well to mix. Store in the jar in the pantry for up to 6 months. Sprinkle on ground beef or chicken as you would any store-bought taco seasoning; also 3 tablespoons = 1 packet of store-bought taco seasoning.

note: Make your own chili powder, onion powder or paprika: Peel onion or garlic and cut into ¼-inch slices. Slice peppers in half and remove the seeds.

Place on a dehydrator tray or parchment-paper–lined baking sheet and place in the dehydrator or oven (at lowest setting). Let dehydrate/bake for several hours (or up to 24 in a dehydrator), until completely dried and brittle enough to break into pieces by hand. The time will vary based on the method used. If using a parchment-paper–lined sheet in the oven, flip the pieces over several times during the process to speed up the drying. When finished, blend each spice individually in a food processor or high-powered blender until a fine powder is achieved. Store in an airtight container at room temperature for up to 6 months or freeze for up to 2 years.

italian seasoning

TOTAL TIME 5 min.   ACTIVE TIME 5 min.   MAKES 2 cups

½ cup dried basil

½ cup dried marjoram

½ cup dried oregano

¼ cup dried rosemary, finely chopped

¼ cup dried thyme

2 tablespoons garlic powder (optional; you may prefer to omit it if you often cook with fresh garlic)

Place the basil, marjoram, oregano, rosemary, thyme, and garlic powder, if using, in a 16-ounce airtight jar with a lid and shake well to mix. Great in any Italian recipe, such as eggplant or chicken Parmesan, Dairy-Free Upside-Down Pizza (page 147), Meatball-Stuffed Spaghetti Squash (page 162), Italian Red Pepper Pot Roast (page 191), and many more.

ragin' cajun seasoning

TOTAL TIME 5 min. | ACTIVE TIME 5 min. | MAKES 1½ cups

½ cup paprika (see Note, page 297)

⅓ cup Himalayan or other sea salt

¼ cup garlic powder

2 tablespoons onion powder (see Note, page 297)

2 tablespoons freshly ground black pepper

1 tablespoon ground cayenne pepper, or to taste (optional)

2 tablespoons dried oregano

1 tablespoon dried thyme

Place the paprika, salt, garlic powder, onion powder, pepper, cayenne, if using, oregano, and thyme in a 10-ounce or larger airtight jar with a lid and shake well to mix. Store in the jar in the pantry for up to 6 months or freeze for up to 2 years. Good on stir-fries, eggs, casseroles, and poultry.

dried ranch dressing mix

TOTAL TIME 5 min. | ACTIVE TIME 5 min. | MAKES ½ cup

¼ cup dried parsley

1 tablespoon dill

1 tablespoon garlic powder

1 tablespoon onion powder (see Note, page 297)

½ teaspoon basil (optional)

½ teaspoon freshly ground black pepper

Place the parsley, dill, garlic powder, onion powder, basil, if using, and pepper in an 8-ounce airtight glass jar with a lid and shake well to mix. Store in the jar in the pantry for 6 months or freeze for up to 2 years.

To make into ranch dressing, mix 1 tablespoon of this mix with ⅓ cup Homemade Mayonnaise (page 320) or plain Greek yogurt and ¼ cup Coconut Milk (page 278).

homemade lemon-pepper seasoning

TOTAL TIME 1 hr. 10 min.   ACTIVE TIME 5 min.   MAKES ½ cup

Zest from 4 to 6 organic lemons or ½ cup dried store-bought

6 tablespoons whole peppercorns (if you're zesting your own lemons) or freshly ground black pepper (if you're using dried store-bought zest)

5 tablespoons Himalayan or other sea salt

If you zested your own lemons, preheat the oven to the lowest setting. Spread out the zest on a baking sheet and place in the oven for about 70 minutes, or until completely dried. Remove from the oven, let cool, then mix well with the peppercorns and salt in a food processor.

If you're using dried store-bought zest, just mix all the ingredients in a food processor. Store in an 8-ounce airtight jar in the pantry for up to 6 months.

seasoned salt

TOTAL TIME 5 min.   ACTIVE TIME 5 min.   MAKES 1 cup

¼ cup onion powder (see Note, page 297)

¼ cup garlic powder

¼ cup freshly ground black pepper

3 tablespoons paprika (see Note, page 297)

2 tablespoons chili powder (see Note, page 297)

2 tablespoons dried parsley (optional)

1 tablespoon red pepper flakes (optional)

Place the onion powder, garlic powder, pepper, paprika, chili powder, and, if using, the parsley and red pepper flakes in an 8-ounce airtight jar with a lid and shake well to mix. Store in the jar in the pantry for up to 6 months.

fajita seasoning

TOTAL TIME 5 min. **ACTIVE TIME** 5 min. **MAKES** ¾ cup

¼ cup chili powder (see Note, page 297)

2 tablespoons sea salt

2 tablespoons paprika (see Note, page 297)

1 tablespoon onion powder (see Note, page 297)

1 tablespoon garlic powder

1 tablespoon ground cumin

1 teaspoon ground cayenne pepper (optional)

Place the chili powder, salt, paprika, onion powder, garlic powder, cumin, and the cayenne, if using, in an 8-ounce airtight jar with a lid and shake well to mix. Store in the jar in the pantry for up to 6 months. This seasoning adds great fajita flavor to any meats, vegetables, or soups. Also great on fajita salads.

chili seasoning mix

TOTAL TIME 5 min. **ACTIVE TIME** 5 min. **MAKES** 1½ cups

½ cup chili powder (see Note, page 297)

¼ cup ground cumin

¼ cup garlic powder

3 tablespoons onion powder (see Note, page 297)

¼ cup dried oregano

2 tablespoons paprika (see Note, page 297)

1 tablespoon dried thyme

Place all the ingredients in a 16-ounce airtight jar with a lid and shake well to mix. Store in the jar in the pantry for up to 6 months. Great for all types of chili.

french onion soup mix

TOTAL TIME 5 min. | **ACTIVE TIME** 5 min. | **MAKES** ¾ cup

½ cup dried onion flakes

1 teaspoon onion powder (see Note, page 297)

1 teaspoon garlic powder

1 teaspoon dried parsley

1 teaspoon Himalayan or other sea salt (optional)

1 teaspoon ground turmeric (optional)

½ teaspoon celery salt

½ teaspoon freshly ground black pepper

Place the onion flakes, onion powder, garlic powder, parsley, salt, if using, turmeric, if using, celery salt, and pepper in an 8-ounce airtight jar with a lid and shake well to mix. Store in the jar in the pantry for up to 6 months. Use approximately ¼ cup per 2 cups beef broth to make French onion broth.

To use as a dried soup mix, you can add ½ cup soy- and MSG-free beef bouillon powder and use as you would a packet of French onion soup mix (¼ cup = 1 package). Excellent on roasts or as a meat seasoning.

herbes de provence

TOTAL TIME 5 min.   **ACTIVE TIME** 5 min.   **MAKES** 1 cup

Zest from 1 organic orange or 2 teaspoons dried store bought (optional)

1 teaspoon lightly ground dried lavender flowers (optional)

½ cup dried thyme

¼ cup dried marjoram

2 tablespoons dried rosemary

2 tablespoons dried savory

1 teaspoon ground fennel

If you zested your own orange, if using, preheat the oven to the lowest setting. Spread out the zest on a baking sheet and place in the oven for about 70 minutes, or until completely dried. Remove from the oven and let cool. Place in a food processor, add the lavender flowers, if using, and lightly pulse.

Remove to a 16-ounce airtight jar with a lid, add the thyme, marjoram, rosemary, savory, and fennel, and shake well to mix. If using dried store-bought zest, just mix all the ingredients in the jar. Excellent in soups, on chicken, or on roasted vegetables.

jamaican jerk seasoning

TOTAL TIME 5 min.   **ACTIVE TIME** 5 min.   **MAKES** ½ cup

¼ cup onion powder (see Note, page 297)

2 tablespoons sea salt

2 tablespoons dried thyme

1 tablespoon ground cinnamon

1 teaspoon ground cayenne pepper (optional)

2 teaspoons ground allspice

Place the onion powder, salt, thyme, cinnamon, cayenne, if using, and allspice in an 8-ounce airtight jar with a lid and shake well to mix. Store in the pantry for up to 6 months. This is especially good if mixed with honey and brushed on meats, such as chicken, before grilling.

asian five-spice seasoning

TOTAL TIME 5 min.   **ACTIVE TIME** 5 min.   **MAKES** ½ cup

2 tablespoons ground anise

1 tablespoon freshly ground black pepper

1 tablespoon ground fennel

1 tablespoon ground cinnamon

1 tablespoon ground cloves

1 tablespoon Himalayan or other sea salt

Place all the ingredients in an 8-ounce airtight jar with a lid and shake well to mix. Store in the jar in the pantry for up to 6 months. Great for recipes like beef and broccoli stir-fry and other Asian dishes.

pumpkin pie spice

TOTAL TIME 5 min.   **ACTIVE TIME** 5 min.   **MAKES** ⅓ cup

¼ cup ground cinnamon

2 teaspoons ground nutmeg

2 teaspoons ground allspice

1 teaspoon ground ginger

½ teaspoon ground cloves
(optional)

Place the cinnamon, nutmeg, allspice, ginger, and cloves, if using, in an 8-ounce airtight jar with a lid and shake well to mix. Store in the jar in the pantry for up to 6 months.

Use as you would regular pumpkin pie spice. Great in pumpkin cheesecake, pumpkin pie, spiced pumpkin lattes, or coconut flour pumpkin muffins.

tangy greek dressing

TOTAL TIME 5 min.   **ACTIVE TIME** 5 min.   **MAKES** ⅔ cup

½ cup olive oil

2 tablespoons red wine vinegar

Small squirt of Dijon mustard

1 garlic clove, crushed

½ teaspoon dried oregano

½ teaspoon dried marjoram

Salt and freshly ground black pepper to taste

Place all the ingredients in a small jar with a lid and shake vigorously to mix. Store in an airtight container in the refrigerator for up to 1 week.

Great with dark lettuces, feta cheese, olives, cucumbers, and cucumber and onion salads.

restaurant-style
tartar sauce

TOTAL TIME 5 min.   **ACTIVE TIME** 5 min.   **MAKES** 1¼ cups

Tartar sauce is another versatile condiment that every mom and amateur chef should have in her arsenal. This one uses delicious homemade mayo, fresh dill pickles, and spices for a flavorful and healthful addition to fish and other dishes.

1 cup Homemade Mayonnaise (page 320)

1 dill pickle, finely minced

¼ medium carrot, finely grated

½ teaspoon dry mustard

1 teaspoon lemon juice

½ teaspoon salt

½ teaspoon freshly ground black pepper

Place all the ingredients in a medium bowl and stir to combine. Store leftovers in an airtight glass container in the refrigerator for up to 1 week.

creamy homemade caesar dressing

TOTAL TIME 10 min.　**ACTIVE TIME** 10 min.　**MAKES** ⅓ cup

1 egg yolk, at room temperature (very important it is not cold!)

2 teaspoons apple cider vinegar

½ teaspoon mustard or dry powder

1 tablespoon fresh lemon juice

2 garlic cloves, finely crushed

2 teaspoons Worcestershire sauce

2 tablespoons grated Parmesan cheese

Salt and freshly ground black pepper to taste

⅓ cup olive oil

In a small bowl, whisk the egg yolk until creamy. Whisk in the vinegar, mustard, lemon juice, garlic, Worcestershire sauce, Parmesan, and salt and pepper. Slowly add the oil, whisking constantly until well blended. If the dressing doesn't incorporate well, your egg might still have been too cold!

Let the entire mixture warm at room temperature for another 10 minutes and attempt to whisk again. Store in an airtight container in the refrigerator for up to 1 week.

Great with dark lettuces, chicken dishes, and asparagus.

RASPBERRY VINAIGRETTE
DRESSING, PAGE 311

CREAMY HOMEMADE
CAESAR DRESSING, PAGE 307

DRIED RANCH
DRESSING MIX,
PAGE 299

TANGY GREEK
DRESSING, PAGE 305

ASIAN FIVE-SPICE
SEASONING, PAGE 304

BALSAMIC VINAIGRETTE
DRESSING, PAGE 312

ZESTY ITALIAN
DRESSING, PAGE 310

FRENCH DRESSING,
PAGE 311

zesty italian dressing

TOTAL TIME 10 min.   ACTIVE TIME 10 min.   MAKES ½ cup

3 tablespoons white wine vinegar

Small squirt of Dijon mustard

¼ cup olive oil

½ teaspoon onion powder (see Note, page 297)

1 to 2 garlic cloves, finely minced

½ teaspoon dried thyme

½ teaspoon dried basil

½ teaspoon dried oregano

Salt and freshly ground black pepper to taste

Place all the ingredients in a small jar with a lid and shake vigorously to mix. Store in an airtight container in the refrigerator for up to 1 week.

Great with any salad or on meat or grilled vegetables as a marinade.

sweet asian dressing

TOTAL TIME 10 min.   ACTIVE TIME 10 min.   MAKES ½ cup

⅓ cup olive oil

3 tablespoons apple cider vinegar

2 teaspoons coconut aminos

2 teaspoons honey

½ teaspoon minced peeled fresh ginger or pinch of ground ginger

½ teaspoon Asian Five-Spice Seasoning (page 304)

Place all the ingredients in a small jar with a lid and shake vigorously to mix. Store in an airtight container in the refrigerator for up to 1 week.

Great with sesame chicken (as a marinade and dipping sauce), spinach salads with cashews, cauliflower, fried rice.

raspberry vinaigrette dressing

TOTAL TIME 10 min. ACTIVE TIME 10 min. MAKES 1 cup

½ cup white wine vinegar

¼ cup olive oil

¼ cup fresh or frozen raspberries

2 teaspoons honey

Place all the ingredients in a blender and blend for 1 minute on high, until smooth. Store leftovers in an airtight container in the refrigerator for up to 1 week.

Great with salads with feta and cashews, grilled chicken salad, and pork as a marinade.

french dressing

TOTAL TIME 10 min. ACTIVE TIME 10 min. MAKES ⅔ cup

⅓ cup olive oil

¼ cup white wine vinegar

1 teaspoon (small squirt) of Dijon mustard

1 tablespoon tomato paste

1 tablespoon honey (optional)

Small chunk of fresh onion or ½ teaspoon onion powder (see Note, page 297)

Place all the ingredients in a blender and blend for 1 minute on high, until smooth. Store in an airtight container in the refrigerator for up to 1 week.

Great with any type of salad (I like it on chef salads), vegetables for dipping.

balsamic vinaigrette dressing

TOTAL TIME 10 min.　　ACTIVE TIME 10 min.　　MAKES 1 cup

½ cup olive oil

⅓ cup balsamic vinegar

1 garlic clove, finely minced

Small squirt of Dijon mustard

1 tablespoon honey (optional)

Salt and freshly ground black pepper to taste

½ teaspoon dried basil or to taste

Place the oil, vinegar, garlic, mustard, honey, if using, salt and pepper, and basil in a small jar with a lid and shake vigorously to mix. Store in an airtight container in the refrigerator for up to 1 week.

Great with any type of salad or beef, chicken, and pork as a marinade.

honey mustard

TOTAL TIME 5 min. | **ACTIVE TIME** 5 min. | **MAKES** 1 cup

I always thought I didn't like honey mustard sauce when I'd only tried store-bought or fast-food versions as a kid. When I finally got the chance to try the real thing at a farm-to-table restaurant, I fell in love and promptly worked on creating my own version that has now become a favorite at our house.

½ cup **Homemade Mayonnaise (page 320)**

¼ cup **Dijon mustard**

¼ cup **raw honey**

½ teaspoon **sea salt**

½ teaspoon **freshly ground black pepper**

¼ teaspoon **garlic powder (optional)**

In a small bowl, whisk together the mayo, mustard, honey, salt, pepper, and, if using, the garlic powder until smooth. Store leftovers in an airtight container in the refrigerator for up to 1 week.

homemade ketchup

TOTAL TIME 2 hr.   **ACTIVE TIME** 10 min.   **MAKES** 2 cups

Ketchup is a magic condiment for kids. Mine will eat almost anything drizzled in ketchup, and this homemade version is simple to make and just as delicious as store-bought without the excess sweeteners.

1 teaspoon chia seeds, for thickening (optional)

3 6-ounce cans tomato paste

½ cup apple cider vinegar

1 teaspoon garlic powder

1 tablespoon onion powder (see Note, page 297)

2 tablespoons raw honey or cane sugar, or ½ teaspoon stevia

2 tablespoons molasses

1 teaspoon sea salt

1 teaspoon dry mustard

Pinch of ground cinnamon

Pinch of ground cloves

Pinch of ground allspice

Pinch of ground cayenne pepper

1 cup filtered water

Process the chia seeds, if using, in a food processor or blender on high speed for about 30 seconds, until they form a fine powder. Add the tomato paste, vinegar, garlic powder, onion powder, honey, molasses, salt, dry mustard, cinnamon, cloves, allspice, cayenne, and water and blend on high for 2 to 3 minutes, until completely smooth.

Remove to a quart-size airtight glass jar with a lid and place in the refrigerator for at least 2 hours to let the flavors meld before serving. Store in an airtight glass jar in the refrigerator for up to 2 weeks.

perfect hollandaise sauce

| TOTAL TIME 15 min. | ACTIVE TIME 10 min. | MAKES ¾ cup |

Hollandaise is one of my favorite sauces to add to fish, vegetables, and breakfast dishes. This homemade version is packed with beneficial fats and flavor!

8 tablespoons (1 stick) unsalted butter

4 egg yolks

3 teaspoons lemon juice

½ teaspoon sea salt

½ teaspoon freshly ground black pepper

In a small saucepan over medium heat, melt the butter and set aside.

In a medium bowl, whisk together the egg yolks, lemon juice, and salt and pepper until smooth. Put the bowl with the egg yolks on the top of a double boiler over simmering water. Whisk the yolks constantly while slowly adding in the melted butter. Once well incorporated, continue to whisk for another 2 to 3 minutes, until the sauce starts to thicken.

Use immediately, or remove from the heat and cover until serving. If it thickens or starts to separate, mix in ½ teaspoon or so of warm water before serving. Best if used immediately, but leftovers can be stored for about 24 hours in the refrigerator and reheated in a small saucepan over low heat, whisking constantly.

satay dipping sauce (peanut-free)

TOTAL TIME 5 min. | **ACTIVE TIME** 5 min. | **MAKES** ½ cup

This peanut-free "peanut" satay sauce goes great with chicken and other dishes. I especially love it with Chicken Satay Skewers (page 161). If you tolerate peanut butter, you can absolutely make this with the real thing, but our family actually prefers this alternative!

¼ cup **SunButter or cashew butter**

2 tablespoons **honey**

2 tablespoons **coconut aminos**

Zest and juice of 1 organic lime

½ teaspoon **fish sauce**

1 teaspoon **garlic powder**

Place all the ingredients in a blender and puree until smooth. Store leftovers in a small airtight container in the refrigerator for up to 1 week.

cranberry sauce

TOTAL TIME 4 hr. 30 min.   **ACTIVE TIME** 15 min.   **MAKES** 2 cups

Cranberry sauce was a holiday staple at our house when I was growing up, but we only ever had the store-bought canned version. A few years after I got married, I had the chance to host Thanksgiving for both sides of the family (no pressure!). I found a recipe for homemade cranberry sauce in an old cookbook at the library and adapted it to remove the refined sugar and to include other fruits for flavoring. The pineapple juice especially adds depth of flavor to this recipe!

1 12-ounce bag fresh or frozen cranberries

½ cup pineapple or orange juice

¼ cup applesauce (no sugar added)

Zest and juice of ½ orange

2 tablespoons honey, or to taste

Place the cranberries, pineapple juice, applesauce, and ¼ cup water in a small saucepan and bring to a boil. Reduce the heat to medium, stirring constantly until the cranberries start to burst, 10 to 15 minutes. Reduce the heat to a simmer and add the orange zest and juice and honey over the cranberry mixture. Simmer for 10 to 15 minutes and remove from the heat.

Cool completely and store in the refrigerator at least 4 hours but preferably overnight before serving. Store leftovers in an airtight glass container for up to 1 week.

tip: This is not as sweet as store-bought versions! Taste at the end of cooking. It is naturally sweet from the fruit juices and applesauce, but you can add more honey to taste if desired.

easy marinara sauce from fresh tomatoes

TOTAL TIME 2 hr. 30 min. | **ACTIVE TIME** 30 min. | **MAKES** 5 to 6 cups

A wonderful recipe to make in the warm summer months when tomatoes are inexpensive and abundant. I often can dozens of jars of this sauce when our garden is in full swing and save them for cooler months as the base for pastas, soups, and casseroles! It's a little time intensive, so I like to devote a day to making and canning big batches.

¼ cup olive oil or tallow

3 medium onions, diced

8 garlic cloves, or more to taste, finely minced

1 carrot, one half grated

5 pounds fresh tomatoes, peeled and seeded (see Note)

⅓ cup finely chopped fresh basil

2 sprigs of parsley or 1 teaspoon dried

1 sprig of fresh thyme or ½ teaspoon dried

1 sprig of fresh oregano or 1 teaspoon dried

2 bay leaves

1 teaspoon sea salt

In a large stockpot over medium heat, pour the oil. Add the onions, garlic, and grated carrot. Sauté for 3 to 5 minutes, until the onions are translucent and tender. Add the tomatoes, basil, parsley, thyme, oregano, bay leaves, and salt. Simmer on low heat for 2 to 3 hours, or until cooked down and starting to darken. Add the carrot piece for the last 30 minutes to absorb acidity. When the tomatoes are soft and easily fall apart when stirred and the carrot has gotten fork-tender, remove the sprigs of herbs and piece of carrot. If you prefer a smooth sauce, use an immersion blender to puree the sauce; skip this step if you like a thick sauce.

Store the leftover sauce in the refrigerator for 1 week, or can it according to your canner's instructions for tomato products.

Note: To peel tomatoes, bring a large pot of water to a boil. One by one, add the tomatoes and remove immediately to an ice-water bath. Once they are cool enough to handle, the skin should peel easily by hand. Peel all the tomatoes and set aside.

homemade mayonnaise

TOTAL TIME 10 min.   ACTIVE TIME 10 min.   MAKES 1¼ cups

Mayo is a universal condiment that makes everything better, in my opinion. In fact, thanks to my small amount of French ancestry, one of my favorite special treats is homemade french fries dipped in homemade mayo!

2 eggs, at room temperature (It is vital that they are room temperature!)

1 teaspoon fresh lemon juice

1 tablespoon white vinegar

½ teaspoon dry mustard

½ teaspoon coarse sea salt

½ cup light olive oil

½ cup refined coconut oil, at room temperature (without coconut flavor or smell), or a more light olive oil (if you don't have or can't tolerate coconut oil)

Place the eggs, lemon juice, vinegar, dry mustard, and salt in a blender (or you can place the ingredients in a small bowl and use an immersion blender). With the blender on high speed, slowly add the oils, starting with a drop at a time and then in a slow stream. Continue until all the oil is added and the mayo is thoroughly blended, about 2 minutes. Store leftovers in an airtight glass jar in the refrigerator for up to 2 weeks.

chipotle-lime mayo

Make the basic mayo recipe and at the end of blending, add 2 cans chipotle peppers and 1 teaspoon fresh lime juice and blend until smooth. Alternatively, you can add 1 teaspoon chili powder instead of the chipotle peppers, but give the flavors at least 30 minutes to meld before serving.

curried mayo

Make the basic mayo recipe and at the end of blending, add 2 teaspoons curry powder.

garlic aioli mayo

Make the basic mayo recipe and at the end of blending, add 2 very finely minced garlic cloves and an extra teaspoon of fresh lemon juice.

garden mayo

Make the basic mayo recipe and at the end of blending, stir in by hand 1 tablespoon each of finely minced fresh dill, fresh parsley, and green onion.

italian mayo

Make the basic mayo recipe and at the end of blending, stir in by hand 1 finely minced garlic clove and 1 tablespoon each of fresh parsley, fresh basil, and fresh oregano.

soy-free homemade
teriyaki

TOTAL TIME 5 min.   **ACTIVE TIME** 5 min.   **MAKES** 1½ cups

Teriyaki is a versatile marinade, dipping sauce, and the base of many dressings, and it is very simple to make. This flavorful homemade version doesn't depend on overly sweet refined sugar, and it adds depth with fresh spices and orange zest.

1 cup coconut aminos

Zest and juice of 1 organic orange

4 garlic cloves, finely minced

2 tablespoons honey, or more to taste

1 tablespoon finely grated fresh peeled ginger

½ teaspoon salt

½ teaspoon white pepper

¼ cup rice wine vinegar

In a small bowl, whisk together all the ingredients. Cover and refrigerate for 3 hours to let the flavors meld before using. Store in an airtight container in the refrigerator for up to 3 weeks.

frances's red hot sauce

TOTAL TIME 25 min. | ACTIVE TIME 10 min. | MAKES 1 cup

Growing up, I had a friend named Frances who loved hot sauce on everything. I didn't understand her obsession at the time but have come to love hot sauce myself in the last few years. When our garden overproduced cayenne peppers one year, I was struggling to find ways to preserve them and decided to give hot sauce a try. I've been making this ever since and it always reminds me of my friend Frances and her hot sauce obsession.

20 fresh cayenne peppers, cored and seeded (for an extra hot sauce, leave in some seeds)

1 medium onion, thinly sliced

4 garlic cloves

1½ cups white vinegar

1 teaspoon salt

Bring 1 cup water to a boil in a medium saucepan and add the peppers, onion, and garlic. Reduce to medium-low and simmer for 10 to 15 minutes, until the vegetables have softened and most of the water has evaporated.

Remove the vegetables to a food processor and puree until smooth. Return to the saucepan and add the vinegar and salt. Simmer on medium for another 8 minutes. Ladle through a fine-mesh strainer to remove any remaining bits of pepper skin from the mixture.

Place in an airtight container in the refrigerator and let the flavors meld for 2 days before using. Store leftovers in an airtight container in the refrigerator for up to 1 month.

tzatziki sauce

TOTAL TIME 5 min.   **ACTIVE TIME** 5 min.   **MAKES** 1½ cups

I once had a pregnancy craving for tzatziki sauce and ate an entire batch of this. I didn't feel one bit of remorse, especially since the base is probiotic-packed unsweetened Greek yogurt, mixed with cucumber, spices, and lemon juice. In fact, I often make a double batch at the beginning of the week to use as a salad dressing and atop other dishes throughout the week.

1 cup **Greek yogurt**

1 tablespoon **minced garlic** or
½ teaspoon **garlic powder**

Pinch of salt

1 teaspoon **fresh lemon juice**

1 **cucumber, finely chopped**

Place all the ingredients in a small bowl and stir until combined. Cover and refrigerate for 2 to 3 hours before serving to let the flavors intensify. Store leftovers in an airtight glass container in the refrigerator for up to 4 days.

bbq sauce

TOTAL TIME 1 hr.   ACTIVE TIME 20 min.   MAKES 3 cups

In the south, BBQ sauce flows like ketchup, and, unfortunately, refined sweeteners are often found in both. This recipe packs all the flavor of regular BBQ sauce without the unnecessary sweeteners.

1 tablespoon coconut oil

1 onion

4 garlic cloves

1 cup tomato sauce

1 cup tomato paste

¼ cup raw honey

¼ cup blackstrap molasses

½ cup apple cider vinegar

1 cup Beef Bone Broth (page 154) or store-bought

1 teaspoon freshly ground black pepper

1 teaspoon celery salt

1 teaspoon dry mustard

1 teaspoon paprika (see Note, page 297)

½ teaspoon ground allspice

Pinch of ground cinnamon

Heat the oil in a large saucepan over medium heat. Slice the onion and garlic and add to the pan. Sauté for 5 to 6 minutes, until the onion is browned and caramelized. Reduce the heat to low. Whisk in the tomato sauce, tomato paste, honey, molasses, vinegar, broth, pepper, celery salt, dry mustard, paprika, allspice, and cinnamon. Simmer for at least 1 hour, stirring constantly, until the sauce reduces by a third and the desired flavor and texture is reached. Taste and adjust for seasonings.

Use immediately or store in an airtight container in the refrigerator for up to 2 weeks.

tip: Making a slow cooker recipe like ribs or a roast? Add all of the ingredients except the oil to the slow cooker with the meat and the sauce will cook as the meat does!

bibliography

SUGAR

Ackerman, Z., et al. "Fructose-induced fatty liver disease: Hepatic effects of blood pressure and plasma triglyceride reduction." *Hypertension* 45 (2005): 1012–1018. doi:10.1161/01.HYP.0000164570.20420.67.

Banks, W. A., et al. "Triglycerides induce leptin resistance at the blood-brain barrier." *Diabetes* 53(5) (2004): 1253–1260. http://www.ncbi.nlm.nih.gov/pubmed/15111494.

Conlee, R. K., Lawler, R. M., and Ross, P. E. "Effects of glucose or fructose feeding on glycogen repletion in muscle and liver after exercise or fasting." *Annals of Nutrition & Metabolism*, 31(2) (1987): 126–132. http://www.ncbi.nlm.nih.gov/pubmed/3592616.

Faeh, D., Minehira, K., Schwarz, J., Periasamy, R., Park, S., and Tappy, L. "Effect of fructose overfeeding and fish oil administration on hepatic de novo lipogenesis and insulin sensitivity in healthy men." *Diabetes* 54(7) (2005): 1907–1913. doi:10.2337/diabetes.54.7.1907.

Ouyang, X., et al. "Fructose consumption as a risk factor for non-alcoholic fatty liver disease." *Journal of Hepatology* 48(6) (2008): 993–999. http://dx.doi.org/10.1016/j.jhep.2008.02.011.

Rada, P., Avena, N. M., Hoebel, B. H. "Daily bingeing on sugar repeatedly releases dopamine in the accumbens shell." *Neuroscience* 134(3) (2005): 737–744. doi:10.1016/j.neuroscience.2005.04.043.

Stanhope, K. L., et al. "Consuming fructose-sweetened, not glucose-sweetened, beverages increases visceral adiposity and lipids and decreases insulin sensitivity in overweight/obese humans." *Journal of Clinical Investigation* 119(5) (2009): 1322–1334. http://www.ncbi.nlm.nih.gov/pmc/articles/PMC2673878/.

Zelber–Sagi, S., et al. "Long term nutritional intake and the risk for non-alcoholic fatty liver disease (NAFLD): A population based study." *Journal of Hepatology* 47(5) (2007): 711–717. http://dx.doi.org/10.1016/j.jhep.2007.06.020.

GRAINS

Carrera–Bastos, P., et al. "The western diet and lifestyle and diseases of civilization." *Dovepress* 2011(2) (2011): 15–35. http://dx.doi.org/10.2147/RRCC.S16919.

Cordain, L. "Cereal grains: Humanity's doublé-edged sword. In Simopoulos, A. (ed), "Evolutionary aspects of nutrition and health: Diet, exercise, genetics, and chronic disease." *World Review of Nutrition and Diet* 84 (1999): 19–73. http://www.direct-ms.org/pdf/EvolutionPaleolithic/Cereal%20Sword.pdf.

Fontes–Villalba, M., Carrera-Bastos, P., and Cordain, L. "African hominin stable isotopic data do not necessarily indicate grass consumption." *PNAS Early Edition* (February 2014). http://2iefwlm3f1n81i891vivh3mx7.wpengine.netdna-cdn.com/wp-content/uploads/2014/02/African+Hominin+Stable+Isotopic+Data+Do+Not+Necessarily+Indicate+Grass+Consumption+The+Paleo+Diet.pdf.

Frassetto, L. A., Schloetter, M., Mietus-Synder, M., Morris Jr., R.C., and Sebastian, A. "Metabolic and physiologic improvements from consuming a paleolithic, hunter-gatherer type diet." *European Journal of Clinical Nutrition* 63 (2009): 947–955. http://www.ncbi.nlm.nih.gov/pubmed/19209185.

Freed, D. L. J. "Do dietary lectins cause disease?" *British Medical Journal* 318(7190) (1999): 1023–1024. http://www.ncbi.nlm.nih.gov/pmc/articles/PMC1115436/?tool=pubmed.

Greger, J. L. "Nondigestible carbohydrates and mineral bioavailability." *Journal of Nutrition* 129(7) (1999): 1434S–1435S. http://jn.nutrition.org/content/129/7/1434S.abstract.

Jönsson, T., Olsson, S., Ahrén, B., Bøg–Hansen, T. C., Dole, A., and Lindeberg, S. "Agrarian diet and diseases of affluence—Do evolutionary novel dietary lectins cause leptin resistance?" *BMC Endocrine Disorders* 5 (2005): 10. doi:10.1186/1472-6823-5-10.

Lindeberg S, et al. "A Palaeolithic diet improves glucose tolerance more than a Mediterranean-like diet in individuals with ischaemic heart disease." *Diabetologia* 50(9) (2007): 1795–1807. http://www.ncbi.nlm.nih.gov/pubmed/17583796.

Lund University. "Original Human 'Stone Age' Diet Is Good for People with Diabetes, Study Finds." *ScienceDaily* (June 28, 2007). www.sciencedaily.com/releases/2007/06/070627225459.htm.

Medical College of Georgia. "Scientists Learn More About How Roughage Keeps You 'Regular.'" *ScienceDaily* (August 23, 2006). http://www.sciencedaily.com/releases/2006/08/060823093156.htm.

Melnik, B. C., Schmitz, G., John, S. M., Carrera-Bastos, P., Lindeberg, S., and Cordain, L. "Metabolic effects of milk protein intake strongly depend on pre-existing metabolic and exercise status." *Nutrition & Metabolism* 10 (2013): 60. doi:10.1186/1743-7075-10-60.

O'Keefe, Jr., J. H., Cordain, L., Jones, P. G., and Abuissa, H. "Coronary artery disease prognosis and C-Reactive Protein levels improve in proportion to percent lowering of low-density lipoprotein." *American Journal of Cardiology* 98 (2006): 135–139. http://2iefwlm3f1n81i891vivh3mx7.wpengine.netdna-cdn.com/wp-content/uploads/2014/06/Coronary+Artery+Disease+Prognosis+and+C+Reactive+Protein-Levels+Improve+in+Proportion+to+Percent+Lowering+of+Low+Density+Lipoprotein.pdf.

Suny Downstate Medical Center. "Low-carb diet reduces inflammation and blood saturated fat in metabolic syndrome." *ScienceDaily* (December 4, 2007). www.sciencedaily.com/releases/2007/12/071203091236.htm.

Westman, E. C., et al. "Low-carbohydrate nutrition and metabolism." *American Journal of Clinical Nutrition* 86(2) (2007): 276–284. http://ajcn.nutrition.org/content/86/2/276.full.

Zanchi, C., Di Leo, G., Ronfani, L., Martelossi, S., Not, T., Ventura, A. "Bone metabolism in celiac disease." *Journal of Pediatrics* 152(2) (2008): 262–265. doi:10.1016/j.jpeds.2008.03.003.

VEGETABLE OILS

Calder, P. C. "n-3 polyunsaturated fatty acids, inflammation, and inflammatory diseases." *American Journal of Clinical Nutrition* 83(6) (2006): S1505–S1519. http://ajcn.nutrition.org/content/83/6/S1505.short.

Christakis, G., Rinzler, S. H., Archer, M., and Kraus, A. "Effect of the anti-coronary club program on coronary heart disease risk-factor status." *Journal of the American Medical Association* 198(6) (1966): 597–604. doi:10.1001/jama.1966.03110190079022.

Cordain, L. "Atherogenic potential of peanut oil-based monounsaturated fatty acids diets." (Letter to the Editor.) *Lipids* 33(2) (1998): 229–230. https://s3.amazonaws.com/paleodietevo2/research/Atherogenic+Potential+of+Peanut+Oil+Based+Monounsaturated+Fatty+Acids+Diet+The+Paleo+Diet.pdf.

Cordain, L. "The nutritional characteristics of a contemporary diet based upon paleolithic food groups." *Journal of the American Nutraceutical Association* 5(3) (2002): 15–24. https://s3.amazonws.com/paleodietevo2/research/The+Nutritional+Characteristics+of+a+Contemporary+Diet+Based+Upon+Paleolithic+Food+Groups+The+Paleo+Diet.pdf.

Cordain, L., and M. S. "Ultraviolet radiation represents an evolutionary selective pressure for the south-to-north gradient of the MTHFR 677TT genotype." *American Journal of Clinical Nutrition* 84(5) (2006): 1243. http://ajcn.nutrition.org/content/84/5/1243.full.

Dayton, S., Pearce, M. L., Hashimoto, S., Dixon, W. J., and Tomiyasu, U. "A controlled clinical trial of a diet high in unsaturated fat in preventing complications of atherosclerosis." *Circulation* 40 (1969): 11-1–11-63. doi:10.1161/01.CIR.40.1S2.II-1.

Eaton, S. B., Eaton III, S. B., Sinclair, A. J., Cordain, L., and Mann, N. J. "Dietary intake of long-chain polyunsaturated fatty acids during the paleolithic." In Simopoulos, A.P. (ed.), "The return of omega 3 fatty acids into the food supply: I. Land-based animal food products and their health effects." *World Review of Nutrition and Diet* 83 (1998): 12–23. http://www.direct-ms.org/pdf/EvolutionPaleolithic/Long%20chain%20fatty%20acids.pdf.

Frantz, Jr., I. D., et al. "Test of effect of lipid lowering by diet on cardiovascular risk: The Minnesota Coronary Survey." *Arteriosclerosis, Thrombosis, and Vascular Biology* 9 (1989): 129–135. doi:10.1161/01.ATV.9.1.129.

Ghosh, S., Novak, E. M., Innis, S. M. "Cardiac proinflam-matory pathways are altered with different dietary n-6 linoleic to n-3 -linolenic acid ratios in normal, fat-fed pigs." *American Journal of Physiology–Heart and Circulatory Physiology* 293 (2007): H2919–H2927. doi:10.1152/ajpheart.00324.2007.

Guyenet, S. "Seed oils and body fatness—a problem-atic revisit." (August 21, 2011). http://wholehealthsource.blogspot.com/2011/08/seed-oils-and-body-fatness-problematic.html.

Haigh, M., and Heady, J. A. "Controlled trial of soya-bean oil in myocardial infarction." *Lancet* 2(7570) (1968): 693–699. http://www.thelancet.com/journals/lancet/article/PIIS0140-6736%2868%2990746-0/abstract.

Hibbeln, J. R., Nieminen, L. R, and Lands, W. E. "Increasing homicide rates and linoleic acid consumption among five Western countries, 1961–2000." *Lipids* 39(12) (2004): 1207–1213. http://www.ncbi.nlm.nih.gov/pubmed/15736917.

Hibbeln, J. R., Nieminen, L. R. G., Blasbalg, T. L., Riggs, J. A., and Lands, W. E. M. "Healthy intakes of n-3 and n-6 fatty acids: estimations considering worldwide diversity." *American Journal of Clinical Nutrition* 83(6) (2006): S1483–S1493. http://ajcn.nutrition.org/content/83/6/S1483.abstract.

Kiecolt-Glaser, J. K., Belury, M. A., Porter, K., Bevers-dorf, D. Q., Lemeshow, S., and Glaser, R. "Depressive symptoms, omega-6:omega-3 fatty acids, and inflam-mation in older adults." *Psychosomatic Medicine* 69(3) (2007): 217–224. doi:10.1097/PSY.0b013e3180313a45.

Lands, W. E. M. "Biochemistry and physiology of eicosanoid precursors in cell membranes." *European Heart Journal Supplements* 3(D) (2001): D22–D25. doi:10.1016/S1520-765X(01)90114-2.

Leren, P. "The effect of plasma-cholesterol-lowering diet in male survivors of myocardial infarction: A controlled clinical trial." *Bulletin of the New York Academy of Medicine* 44(8) (1968): 1012–1020. http://www.ncbi.nlm.nih.gov/pmc/articles/PMC1750292/.

Lindenberg, S., Cordain, L., and Eaton, S. B. "Biological and clinical potential of a palaeolithic diet." *Journal of Nutritional & Environmental Medicine* 13(3) (2003): 149–160. https://s3.amazonaws.com/paleodietevo2/research/Biological+and+Clinical+Potential+of+a+Paleolithic+Diet+The+Paleo+Diet.pdf.

de Lorgeril, M., and Salen, P. "New insights into the health effects of dietary saturated and omega-6 and omega-3 polyunsaturated fatty acids." *BMC Medicine* 10 (2012): 50. doi:10.1186/1741-7015-10-50.

Nair, U., Bartsch, H., and Nair, J. "Lipid peroxidation-induced DNA damage in cáncer-prone inflammatory diseases: A review of published adduct types and levels in humans." *Free Radical Biology and Medicine* 43(8) (2007): 1109–1120. http://www.ncbi.nlm.nih.gov/pubmed/17854706.

Ramsden, C. E., Hibbeln, J. R., Majchrzak, S. F., and Davis, J.M. "n-6 fatty acid-specific and mixed polyun-saturate dietary interventions have different effects on CHD risk: a meta-analysis of randomised controlled trials." *British Journal of Nutrition* 104(11) (2010): 1586–1600. doi:10.1017/S0007114510004010.

Rose, G. A., Thomson, W. B., and Williams, R. T. "Corn oil in treatment of ischaemic heart disease." *British Medical Journal* 1(5449) (1965): 1531–1533. http://www.ncbi.nlm.nih.gov/pmc/articles/PMC2166702/.

Simopoulos, A. P. "Evolutionary aspects of diet, the omega-6/omega-3 ratio and genetic variation: nutri-tional implications for chronic diseases." *Biomedicine & Pharmacotherapy* 60(9) (2006): 502–507. doi:10.1016/j.biopha.2006.07.080.

Simopoulos, A. P. "The importance of the ratio of omega-6/omega-3 essential fatty acids." *Biomedi-cine & Pharmacotherapy* 56(8) (2002): 365–379. doi:10.1016/S0753-3322(02)00253-6.

Siri-Tarino, P. W., Sun, Q., Hu, F. B., and Krauss, R. M. "Meta-analysis of prospective cohort studies evaluat-ing the association of saturated fat with cardiovascular disease." *American Journal of Clinical Nutrition* 91(3) (2010): 535–546. doi:10.3945/ajcn.2009.27725.

University of Toronto. "Some 'healthy' vegetable oils may actually increase risk of heart disease." *Science-Daily* (November 11, 2013). www.sciencedaily.com/releases/2013/11/131111122105.htm.

Index